Spiders' Games

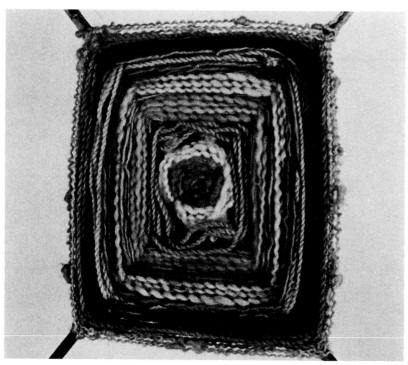

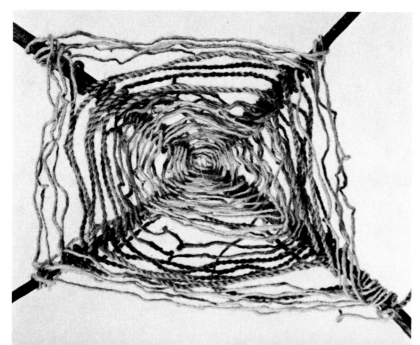

Spiders' Games

A Book for Beginning Weavers

Phylis Morrison

UNIVERSITY OF WASHINGTON PRESS   *Seattle and London*

Library of Congress Cataloging in Publication Data

Morrison, Phylis, 1927-
 Spiders' games.

 1. Hand Weaving. I. Title.
TT848.M675   746.1'4   78-21754
ISBN 0-295-95620-8

Book and jacket design by Audrey Meyer

Photographs from the Peabody Museum of
Archaeology and Ethnology copyright © by
the President and Fellows of Harvard
College.

Drawings and photographs not otherwise
credited are by the author.

Foreword

Both looms "will lead you to
experience the rhythm of weaving, the
dance of the hand and body turning linear
thread into a web of fabric."

Working with threads can be a relatively mindless activity: it is possible to
weave and not really notice what one is doing or know what one could do.
Phylis Morrison, however, is ambitious for us. She requires that we work
with sensitivity and care as we explore structure, texture, color, pattern,
and function. One step at a time, beginning with such elemental play as
winding a ball of thread, she brings us up to the edges and then into the
midst of the rich complexities inherent in woven art. How we then proceed
is up to us, and having been provided here with the tools (of which self-
reliance surely is the most important) we are at once competent and
confident.

It is not easy to describe the ways in which Phylis brings us to this
happy state. A skillful teacher, she has inserted into her text and pictures
those facts which are essential to an understanding of weaving as a
process, and of fiber and dye as the materials of this process. *Spiders'
Games* is, in fact, a scientific book, reminding us of the basic nature of our
materials and how this affects our craft. It then gives us the means to
understand how material and process are integrated in the finished
product.

Of great importance to me are the author's observations about the
tradition: she shares with us her deep understanding of how our activities
are connected to traditions extending well back in time and widespread
around the world, enabling us to touch all of humankind.

Here is a "how-to" weaving book that is beautiful, thriftily practical, and
deeply poetic. Reading *Spiders' Games* I recalled my own childhood
schooling, having to sit still for hours at a time with my hands "folded" on
the desktop. How wonderful it will be for the readers of this book (and
their students) who never will be required to "behave" by folding/locking
their hands/minds. With *Spiders' Games* one is unlocked and truly can
begin.

Joanne Segal Brandford
Ithaca, New York
April 1978

Acknowledgments

A book like this one cannot come to exist without borrowing from the work of many people. I have relied heavily on the knowledge of many weavers whom I never knew, who taught me through the example of their woven cloth. The skill of my own teachers, especially Gretchen Muller and Joanne Brandford, is a strong thread throughout these pages. Many people, including Muffy Paradise, Susan Riecken, Angela Kimberk, Katharine Kvaraceus, and my students gave their ideas and time with generosity. Their participation allowed the book to grow in directions that would have been missing without their help. The anthropologists whose field photographs you see in the book shared their professional research. Museums opened their collections. Readers will find the book far easier to use than it would have been because of the skill of a weaver of words, my editor, Vicki Adams. And there was Phil Morrison, who gave in all the ways I asked, and also in the ways I did not know to ask.

I thank you, each and all.

Contents

These are the hands of two weavers, women from Indonesia. They are passing
a ball of yarn to each other, forming a warp to weave upon. This book offers
the hand, the thread, and the continuation of the old skills to you. (Photograph
by Monni Adams)

The central decoration of the Mexican robe discussed in the chapter on color. These bright, hot colors have a long tradition with those weavers. The loom on which this was woven is similar to looms explored in this book.

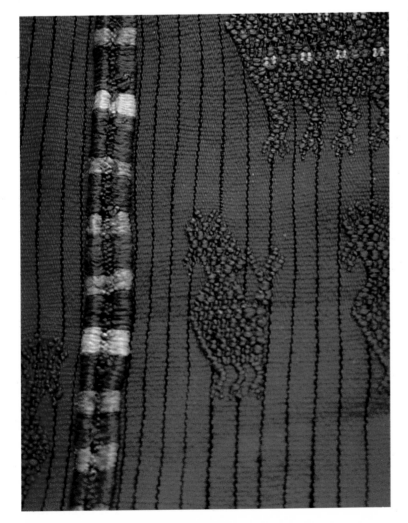

Brocaded birds of a shiny yarn contrast with the matte surface of the red cotton cloth in this Guatemalan shirt. The conspicuous vertical pattern is the embroidered joining of two narrower pieces to make a garment wide enough to wear.

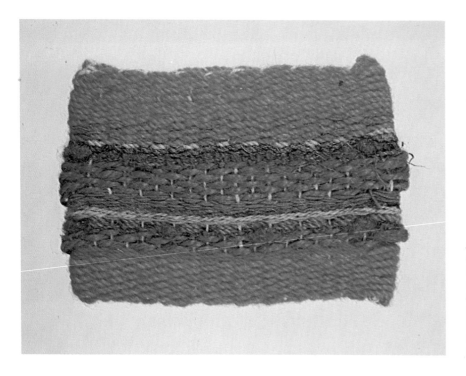

A bag woven with home-dyed yarns by a new weaver, complete as it came off the "loom." The different behavior of different weights and textures of yarn add to the liveliness of this tiny weaving. You can just barely see the loops of warp yarn at the top, open edge of this bag. Chapter 4 explains the process.

Wool yarns of different weights and textures.

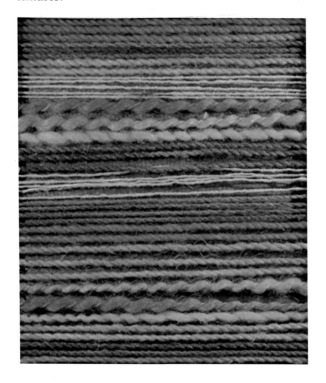

The first work of a new weaver. Two methods for weaving bands such as this one and the Norwegian example are given in Chapter 5.

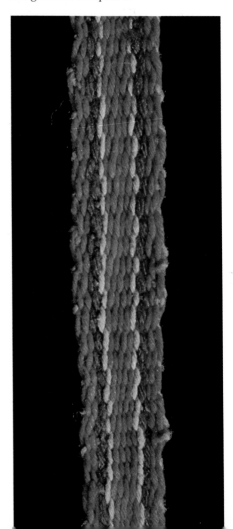

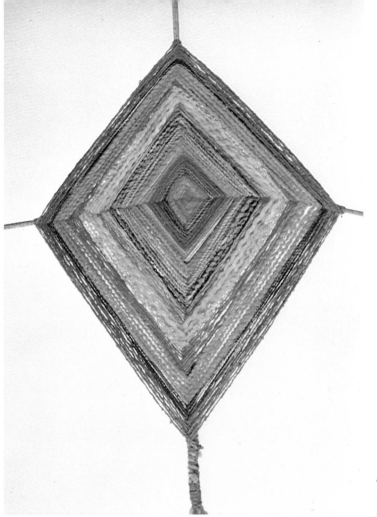

The simple structure of a god's eye makes it an easy place to try out the effects colors have on each other.

This bag, again one woven by a novice, shows a subtle and unusual use of color. The corded finish around the edge of the bag, ending in two simple tassels, made the small project finished and complete.

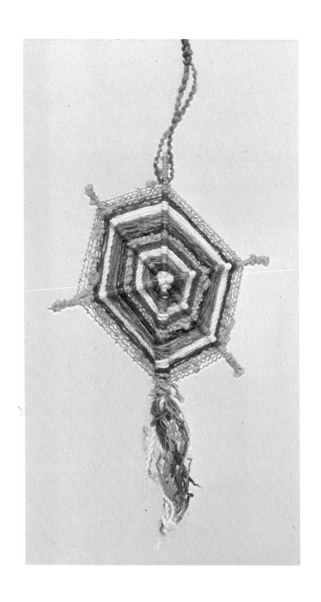

God's eyes.

Another beginner's bag with a zippered closure.

A little zippered bag, tourist goods from Comalapa, Guatemala. These bags, quickly and even carelessly woven, are charming partially because of their shortcomings. Often the small brocaded figures, worked by counting the yarns over which they lie, are distorted in shape from neighbor to neighbor. Casual variation in the spacing of the warp threads caused the differences in the birds you see here.

This traditional pattern of interlocking colors has been discovered by weavers in lands as distant as Ireland and India. Here the band is finished by plying the warp yarns, several at a time, into a thick fringe.

This enlargement of part of a traditional Norwegian band weaving shows the individual yarns as the elements of the pattern.

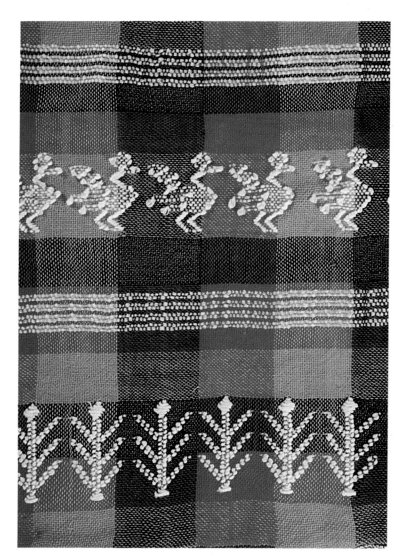

Two ways of producing pattern appear
in this cloth. The plain weave
background is broken up in checkered
squares. The white figures, parades of
birds and rows of maize, are brocade
woven. You will find details of this
Mexican cloth from Chiapas in the
chapter on brocade.

Narrow woven bands of "kente" cloth
from Ghana in Africa. The plain
stripes are weft-faced weaving; the
other patterns are brocade techniques.
Kente cloth always shows clever
combinations of various ways of
making designs.

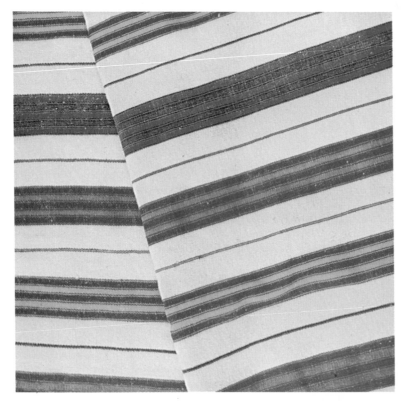

This cloth has no more complicated a
pattern than a stripe, yet it has been
designed with a real understanding of
what is possible. The intense undiluted
color and the sharpness of the
narrowest stripes are due to the fact
that the cloth is warp-faced. Chapters 5
and 8 show how this is done.

On Becoming a Weaver

This book will help you gain a complicated set of skills: some of hand, some of eye, some of judgment—all of them together adding up to mastery of the act of weaving. If you persevere to the book's end, you will be able to plan and give form to any textile you have in mind. You will have learned to notice and to choose yarns, to color them, to handle them with skill, and to weave them into cloth using several different kinds of homemade looms. You will also have learned to control the texture and form of your weaving and to embellish that weaving with your own patterns. Nor do you need to have any previous understanding of weaving or how it is done, for care has been taken to give you useful places to begin.

You are at the heart of this process of making cloth. In the same way as the fiber must first be spun and the wooden yarn beater be made smooth, you must gain some new skills. As you read this book, take time to think things through. Mentally finger your way through the new processes before you actually try them. Be patient with yourself when some skills seem to evade you: other beginners have been this way before you and have mastered what you now find difficult. At every step, let your own imagination tell you what to add to the material product the book shows you: see it glow with your colors, feel its surface take on the texture you wish, shape its use. The more you weave, the more these powers will grow, but you already have their origins within you.

Along with care that the learning needs of beginning weavers will be met has gone an emphasis on self-reliance. This book tries to explain and show each new process in such a way that you will come to understand it well enough to be able to change it for yourself. You should express your own ideas of what is beautiful and interesting as you use every chapter. Additionally, you will become able to see weaving of every kind—whether the product of the machine or that of the hand—with some understanding of how it was made.

This understanding of process will be of especial use to experienced weavers, who already know much of what is presented here, but who may not have before thought through or seen clearly the many details of complex interrelationships over which they are master. This way of knowing might enable such weavers to use their own skills in ways new to them. For those weavers who use this as their first weaving book, a great part of the literature on weaving, both practical material intended for artists and ethnographic material intended for scholars, should become understandable, and thus of practical use.

To care about weaving, to make weavings, is to be in touch with a long human tradition. We people have woven, first baskets and then cloth, for at least ten thousand years. This book will give you many ways to become connected with that tradition. You will find pictures of the weaving of people in other places and in other times. You can learn much of how to weave by studying these examples. You can also begin to learn to recognize the styles of individual cultures. Using the riches in other books, you could come to know more about those people themselves.

The practical tools you will be using, very like those used for thousands of years, will also connect you with the weavers who have come before. You will realize what human ingenuity and skill went into devising the mechanisms that make cloth grow quickly and gracefully. You will touch the weaving and see it change before you in ways that can be known only to weavers and not to users of the finished cloth. Be looking.

Cloth and the basic processes by which it is made have changed astonishingly little over time. Almost all of the industrially woven products of today could have been duplicated with the skills and tools that were available to weavers thousands of years ago. These same skills and tools are still in use among weavers working within traditional cultures today and are available to you. Our powered machines make the same old cloth with a smaller expenditure of human labor, more cheaply and swiftly, but with less personal human intervention.

If you wish it, and persevere in understanding the skills outlined in this book, you can join that company of people who weave new cloths with their hands and caring minds. Whether the cloth you weave will be for functional use or only for delight, whether its structure and design will lie within an old tradition or will be a new experiment is for you to choose. Here is a way to begin.

When brave Theseus was to enter the maze leading into the monster's lair, Ariadne gave him a ball of yarn. One end of the clew she kept. He, unwinding yarn from the ball as he went through the maze, would at least not lose his way. This book will try to be such a thread.

The workbasket of a weaver of long ago, from Peru. (The Peabody Museum of Archaeology and Ethnology. Photograph by Hillel Burger)

10

1. The Single Thread

Look at yarn, thread, rope—anything you imagine could be woven. Feel a strand of it: is it soft, harsh, smooth, rough, or limp? Is it stiff, thin, thick, shimmery, elastic, compressible, or fuzzy? Smell it. Tug it: how strong is it? Rub it. Is it made up of smaller parts? Is it all of a single color?

Has it been twisted? Twist, looking like the spiral on a screw or bolt, tells you that a yarn has been spun. You can gain some insight into what this twist does for yarn by untwisting a strand for a few inches and tugging and rubbing the loosened fibers. Some yarns and ropes first untwist into two or three smaller yarns which can themselves be untwisted further. In most cases you will end up with a fluffy little pile of filaments. You can even crudely twist them back into some semblance of the yarn you started with. There is a good chance these filaments are the growth from the woolly back of a sheep or the tassel that grows on the furry seeds of the cotton plant. Or they could be artificially made fibers that were extruded from a machine in much the same way as threads of garlic from a garlic press. Not all yarns are spun: think of the single long filament in nylon stockings or the individual strands of grass in woven mats or baskets.

Many yarns.

Dissecting a woolen yarn.

This Nigerian woman is spinning cotton. Her thread will be woven into highly valued cloth. The little spindle, turning like a top, twisting the fibers on which it hangs, is one of our oldest machines. The filaments of most yarns are twisted in their making—today by whirring machines, thousands of years ago between finger and thumb. (Photograph by Aylette Jenness)

11

Examine the cloth around you: curtains, winter coats, dishcloths, shirts, and socks. Focus your attention on the yarns they are made of. A magnifying glass, or if you are lucky, a low-power microscope, will show you even more detail than your unaided eye can see. You will be astonished at how much the yarns vary in texture, size, and structure. A thick hempen rope and a delicate sewing thread have the same structure, while other forms are quite unexpected: there are yarns looped, braided, thick and thin by turns! Remember all these possibilities when you are weaving.

Be noticing also in the world about you other materials you could use to weave with: grasses, sticks—anything interesting in color and texture. Begin collecting such things so you will have many materials at hand.

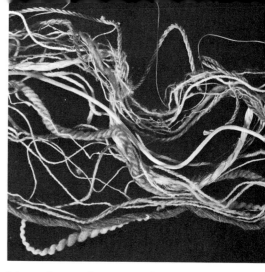

Many sizes and textures of yarn.

The Substances

As you weave, the individual behavior of yarns will make you aware of the various substances of which they are made. It does not matter whether they are the familiar cotton, linen, silk, and wool; the more unusual alpaca, yak, dog, straw, agave, jute, and raffia; or the manmade rayons, nylons, and acrylics. They each act differently. As all the weavers who came before you learned to understand these unique properties, so will you. The properties of these different substances will determine what you can do with the yarns and also how the woven product will behave: a slippery fiber and a stretchy one require different handling and produce different cloths. The more sensitive you are to the behavior of yarn and cloth, noticing effects and thinking through what causes them, the more pleasing will be your results. You will find you already know a great deal; you have been seeing and using woven products all your life.

What To Use

If you have no materials at hand already, get wool yarns to use in your first weavings. Wool has a springy yet resilient quality that makes it very easy to work with. It was one of the first spun yarns and has remained in constant use—a testament to its desirable characteristics. While wool is a good material with which to start, experiment with other materials as well.

Yarns can have different structures. Beginning on the left, these are one-ply, two-ply, three-ply and multiple-ply yarns. The first is twisted, and that is all, while the others are made of several individually twisted strands. The first two are wool, the third cotton, and the fourth jute.

There are many substances with long filaments you might collect to enrich your weaving. Think of grass, jute, string, bamboo, sticks, wire, clothesline.

You do not need many different yarns to start with. If you begin by dyeing yarns to colors you like, as the next chapter suggests, you should start by buying a few textures of white or light-colored yarn. By dyeing these you can have a rainbow of colors, and you will gain skills in handling the yarn during the dyeing process. Again, wool is a good substance to start with, as it dyes richly and easily.

If you are able to buy yarns from a local weavers' store, confer with a knowledgeable salesperson about yarn types that would be good for a beginning collection. If you buy from samples by mail, get some yarn that seems strong, that does not come apart easily when you rub it between thumb and finger. Many two-ply woolens would fit that description. You do not want to use such yarns exclusively, but their predictable good behavior will be an aid as you begin weaving. Do not get too many yarns to start with: you will learn more about what you like as you use these.

But if you have any kind of pleasing yarns on hand around the house, go ahead and try them out. Using them will teach you more than these words can say! It is a mistake to make do with materials you do not like. Your efforts will be wasted on yarns whose color, sheen, and size do not delight you.

Some fibers before they are spun:

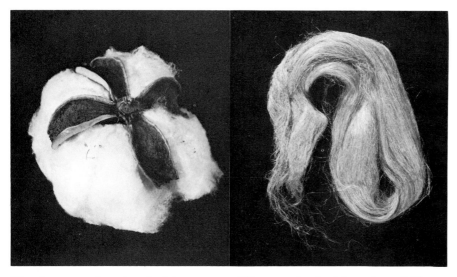

The ripe opened seed pod of the cotton plant.

Filaments leached from the tall fibrous stem of the blue-flowering flax plant, ready to be spun into linen.

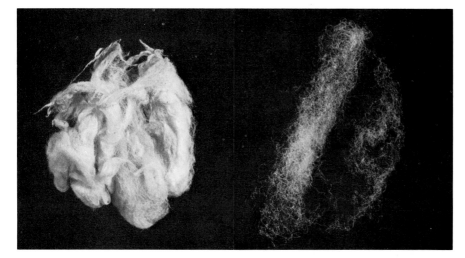

A hank of sheep's wool.

A few filaments of kinky wool, teased out from that hank. The kinkiness affects the properties of woolen cloth, helping it to have and to keep its open, fluffy, soft, elastic qualities. Linen is obviously a very different substance from wool.

Managing the Single Thread

If you were to follow a single fiber from its harvest to the finished manufactured cloth, you would be surprised at how many times the yarn is wound and rewound: for storage, for dyeing and other chemical processing, for plying, for blending, for dressing the loom, for weaving. Much machinery and much time goes into those winding manipulations. This is very noticeable in the mechanized weaving of today, but it is also true of preindustrial weaving. Making skeins and winding balls are the hand processes equivalent to what machines do. Skeins permit the easy access of dye and allow the yarn to be stored under no tension; balls allow for easy access of the running yarn.

To Make a Skein

There are many ways to wind a skein. It can be made by winding around your thumb-pit to your elbow, or around the legs of a chair turned upsidedown. Or you might wind around two sticks firmly planted in the ground—that must surely be an old method!

The old New England weavers had an elegant solution to this problem of making a skein: a simple tool they called a "niddy-noddy," which bobs and nods as you wind your yarn. It is constructed of a staff with end cross-pieces at right angles to each other and winds a skein twice its own length (see the Appendix on Tools for instructions on making one). The niddy-noddy with its skein of yarn wound on is a beautiful form. Stop and look at it from different angles: there are surprises!

When you make any skein, keep track of the beginning of the yarn. When you finish winding, break off the end, and tie it and the beginning together. You need to wind two or three loops of other yarn or string around the skein to hold it roughly in order through whatever processes will now happen to it. The loops will also help in putting the skein back into a ring when you are ready to wind it into balls.

Using a niddy noddy:

 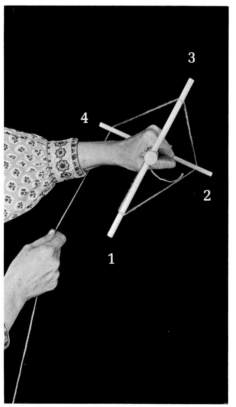 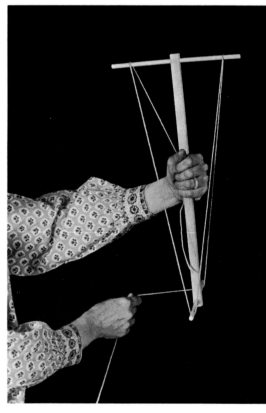

1. *Looking down onto the main staff of a niddy-noddy.*

2. *To start winding on a niddy-noddy, grasp it at its middle, holding the yarn's end in that grasp as well. Think of the four ends of the crossbars as being numbered in turn, as in the photo. Wind your yarn over 1, under 2, over 3, and under 4, then back over the first bar again.*

3. *Continue, following the path of the thread that was laid down the first time around.*

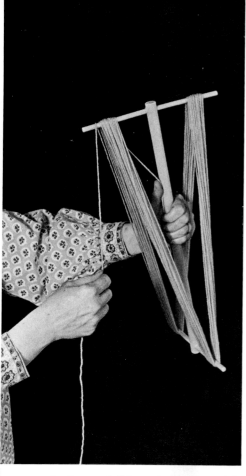

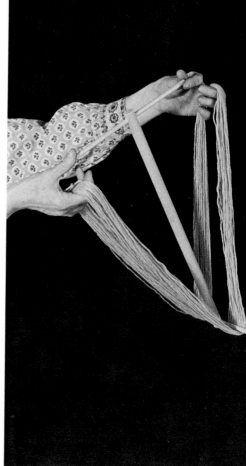

4. As you fall into the rhythm of the winding, the tool will begin to nod. "Niddy-noddy, niddy-noddy All head and no body." (Old rhyme)

5. When you've wound as much as you wish, break off the yarn, and tie the end to the beginning.

6. After you've tied yarn loops around the skein, slip it off the frame.

7. Two yarn loops loosely encircling a skein of wool. One of them is tied to the skein's ends. The best way to pick up a skein is by these loops. This tends to preserve the skein untangled, or, if the skein is in a less-than-neat state, it is the first step toward restoring order. When yarn is wound in a skein, it is easy to determine its length: if a skein is half a yard long from end to end, then one strand is a yard around. Count the number of strands to arrive at the yardage.

Storing yarns, especially wools, in skeins preserves the resiliency, loft, and texture of the yarn. Therefore the loops should not squeeze the skein at all but should be very loose. This is especially important if you are going to dye the skeins, for tight loops would keep the dye from getting at the section of the yarn inside the constriction. (In the next chapter you will find a way to take advantage of this "problem.") Knot one of the loops to the skein's ends; this will make it easy to find the ends when you need them. It is a good idea to pick skeins up by these looped ties, especially when they are wet, so make the loops strong enough for that. The loops are easier to see and find if they contrast with the skein's own yarns.

Everybody occasionally gets into a tangle when working with yarn. When this happens to you, do not panic. Any tangle will dissolve if you start with one end of the yarn and follow the line of the thread, winding as you go, until you reach the other end. Try to keep the messy part as open and loose as you can while you do this. Be patient.

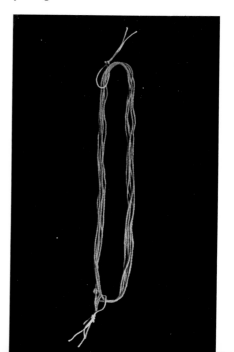

1. There is a lovely way weavers twist a skein into a non-tangling hank for storage in a drawer, or, better yet, in a basket. Hold the skein, a hand at each end, your fingers through the opening. (If the skein's too long, you can make it shorter: cross it in the middle, then fold in half.) With your fingers holding the skein, turn one hand around and around, so that the skein twists up, looking like a tight rope.

2. As the twist tightens, the holes at the skein's end will close up until there is room for only a finger in each. Hold the skein in the middle with your teeth and bring the ends together. When you let go with your teeth, the middle of the skein will begin to twist.

3. If you have put enough turns into the system, the twist will run up the hank to your hands. Slip the end held by one hand into the hole held by the other hand. You'll have made a hank that won't come undone and that will keep the yarn with no tension.

Winding a ball from a skein.

16

To Wind a Ball

The ball is a useful structure because it unwinds easily, giving back the thread inch by inch. There are other structures that perform the same task: yarn comes from the mill on spools or cones; weavers use shuttles to hold and play out the yarn as they need it in the act of weaving; even the sewing needle works as a tool for playing out thread.

Did your grandmother ever get you to hold out your hands, separate and parallel, festoon them with a skein of yarn and wind a ball? Or did you ever, for want of a helper, lay a skein over the back of a chair and proceed to make a ball, perhaps having some problem with tangles in the skein? This was a more universal experience in the past than it is today. If you are lucky, and it was your grandmother who showed you this, then think: surely it was her grandmother who showed her? And back into time your skill must reach, in an unbroken thread to the times when weaving and spinning and ball-winding were invented!

While winding the yarn, remember to see what you are doing: the live moving line of the thread is beautiful to watch. It is a part of weaving known only to the weaver. If you are winding the ball with a friend holding the skein, think how old the process you are sharing is.

It has been many hundreds of years since this ball was wound, yet it looks as though it was made just yesterday. It is part of a cache of working materials that once belonged to a Peruvian weaver. (The Peabody Museum of Archaeology and Ethnology. Photograph by Hillel Burger)

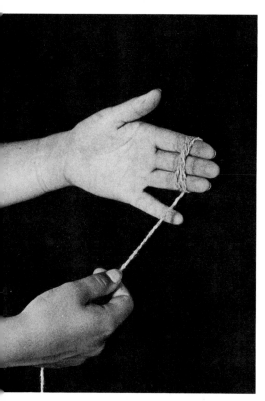

1. To start making a ball, wind the yarn loosely round and round three or four of one hand's fingers.

2. After ten rounds or so, slip your fingers out and wind a few turns around this miniature skein, giving it a wasp waist. Fold it in half at the waist: now you have a somewhat spherical mass. Wind a few turns—it might be ten—around it in some direction. Change direction and wind a few more turns.

3. It is not good for the yarn if the ball becomes hard, as it will if the yarn is wound tightly. The tension on the fibers eventually distorts their internal structure. To wind soft balls, hold the partially wound ball inside your fingers in such a way that you can wind over them. At the end of that series of winding, slip your fingers out and repeat winding in a new direction.

The pattern in this Japanese cloth was formed during the dyeing of the yarns, before the cloth was woven. Sections of the yarn were wound with string ties that the dye did not penetrate. See page 27

A piece of striped Nigerian cloth. One of the stripes is punctuated by a tie-dyed section.

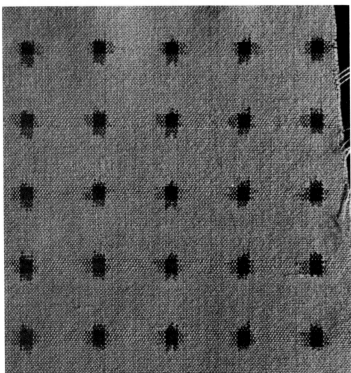

Cloth by this method is called "ikat." This example, appearing as the reverse of the one above it, could have been made by tying every part of the threads except the dark spots.

Another example from Japan, the effect depending on where the pattern crossings occur. These are called double ikats.

2. Color, Color

Just over a hundred years ago, cloth could not be of any color. It could be dyed only with those colors that were nature's bounty; man's ingenuity had not yet made available a palette of all the colors there are. Extracts from plant materials were the usual source of dyestuffs. Which plants would produce relatively permanent colors on cloth was far from obvious. Endless experimentation and observation must have gone into the knowledge of dyeing people held. Blues from indigo were available and loved almost everywhere. The same blue-making molecule, now copied by man, colors our blue jeans. Soft greens and browns were made from everybody's local plants, but colorfast reds and purples were harder to come by and were very expensive. Peoples' clothes and household goods were by necessity and by style limited in palette.

It was not that chemists could not produce many colors. They could, but there is more to a dye than color alone. A dye must first dissolve in water, so that it can reach every small part of the fibers to be dyed; then it must bond to those fibers permanently, suddenly no longer soluble in water. That was a hard trick. It was first successfully done in 1856, in England, with a dyestuff called "mauve." Then followed years in which the color of fashion was that of the newest dye made. The intimate world of people became more and more colorful.

It was an extraordinary transition, affecting people in many ways. In Mexico and Guatemala today, we see woven cloth in a characteristic set of manmade colors: typically pinks, oranges, roses, reds. At first one supposes these gaudy colors go back only to the time when naive craftsmen were suddenly freed from the limits of their original palette.

It is not so. Long before then, those people had gathered a little insect that lived on a local cactus. The body of this insect, the cochineal bug, was used to dye fibers just that same set of colors: oranges, hot pinks, magentas, cerises. It would appear that the newly available dyes were used to reproduce the traditional range of colors Mexican weavers still love today.

Like those craftsmen, you can make your own choices. The availability of color in a packet lets you have as varied a palette as you wish, with colors relating to each other as subtly or as boldly as your mind's eye suggests. A little organization can make the labor of dyeing much less than you would suppose, and full of satisfying adventure. The cost of dyestuffs is small, and dyeing permits the frugal buying of only a few different yarns, yet yields a rainbow of colors.

Thinking about Color

Whether you dye your yarns or buy them in pleasing colors, you need to be thoughtful about the way color works in textiles. Colors can be mixed in two very different ways: molecule by molecule, as when two liquid dyes are stirred together; or by juxtaposing different colors of yarns, and letting the "mixing" occur in the eye of the beholder. In each case, the resultant color has some of the qualities of each of its parents. When colors are mixed by juxtaposition, some unusual effects are produced. As those varied yarns are woven together, the bits of color are seen both separately and blended: the cloth has one aspect seen from nearby, another at a distance. The angle at which the cloth is seen also affects such woven

A Mexican robe woven from native brown cotton and many-hued dyed yarns. Look in the color plates to see a detail of this robe.

color. The Pointillist painters explored these ideas with paints; for many weavers such explorations become one of the inherent rewards of weaving. The more you understand color and the more you think about it, the more you will enrich the experience of weaving for yourself and the more you will see in the weaving of others.

Play with colors in many ways. Save magazine photographs containing interesting color relationships. Cut them into long strips and reassemble the parts, to see what happens to the colors when you no longer see the picture's subject matter. Notice and remember color ranges in nature, in museums, in peoples' clothing. Make bouquets.

To explore freely what happens when colors are made by mixing, mess about with a set of food colors from the grocery store. Fill several clear, colorless glasses with water and add the colors, single drop by single drop. Let the colors mix slowly, swirling into each other and the water before your eyes. A white surface—it can be a piece of paper—in a brightly lit or sunny spot is the best place to set the glasses on. A very rough rule of thumb for any mixing of colors suggests that most pairs of colors mixed give you a bright color, while any three colors, in various proportions, give you softer, subdued ones. Strength and paleness of color always depend upon dilution in some way. Watch what happens and make your own sense of it: what you come to understand for yourself is knowledge you can use.

Often you will make one color to start with and then change it to another through a series of transitions, each stage related to the one before. Such a series of colors can be very satisfactory in a woven piece, so remember that process when you come to dye.

After you have dyed yarns, study them to learn more about their color relationships. Place them in different groupings and juxtapositions. There are weavers whose product seems to be nothing but baskets filled with balls of many colors, like bouquets of flowers.

Not yet a weaving, a basket of various colors and textures of yarn is a rewarding step along the way.

Dyestuffs

It will be much easier to dye your yarns a specific color if you understand something of how the dyestuffs work and if you organize them so they are convenient to use. This book will discuss dyeing with ordinary household dyes, those little packets of color available at drug, grocery, and variety stores. The general principles of their use are the same as for other dyes, both natural and manmade.

Household dyes are a mixture of several different dye chemicals. Not every fiber can be united to every dye: as a class, animal fibers behave very differently from plant fibers. Many synthetic fibers behave either like those from plants or like those from animals: rayon acts like a plant fiber—it is, in fact, cellulose—and nylon acts like animal stuff—it is very similar to protein in its structure. Some act like neither, different in their dye affinities from anything else. Generally, wools are very easy to dye, cottons are not quite so amenable. The manufacturers of all-purpose dyes have put substances into their mixture that will color various fibers. Because each of these colorants is a different chemical, different fibers may not dye to the same color in the same dyebath. If you tie wool skeins with cotton ties, you'll notice this effect: you may even want to make test dyeings with different yarns.

Plant Fibers		Animal Fibers		Synthetics
cotton	sisal	wool	angora	nylon
linen	(rayon)	silk	camel	rayon
jute		mohair	(nylon)	dacron
hemp		alpaca		acrylics

When you use household dyes, there is always some dye left in the dyebath: if you are dyeing wool, you may have used up all the animal-fiber loving dye, but the dyebath will still be strongly colored by the plant-reacting dye that is there. You have to rinse that dye carefully out of your yarn when you have finished dyeing.

In contrast to household dyes are specialized dyes made of only one ingredient which are usually useful with only one class of fibers, as "acid" dyes with wool or "fiber-reactive" dyes with cotton. It is possible when using them to end up with an entirely clear dyebath. More information about them is contained in the list of suppliers and the bibliography in the Appendix on Tools.

Many packages of household dyes also contain salt. While salt does not enter into the bond between dyestuff and fiber, there is an interesting reason for its presence which you can take advantage of. In the dyepot are molecules of water and dye, as well as the fibers of yarn. As long as the water contains many dye molecules, they attach themselves to the fiber at a good rate. That rate slows down when most of the dye has left the solution, but the addition of salt to the water can "crowd" the dye molecules out, speeding up the dyeing process again. You can use your understanding of this to control the rate of what happens in your dyepots. The heat of a dye solution also affects the rate of dyeing: what would take days to happen at room temperature can happen in an hour at simmering heat.

All of the brands of household dyes seem to work well—find your own favorites. Just four colors of dye, red, yellow, blue and black, will let you mix many more colors of your own. (Some people prefer to start with magenta, royal blue, turquoise, yellow, and black.) Experiment for yourself: mix small batches of dye, and color small amounts of wool while you learn to control the colors.

Organizing the Dyestuffs

Any kitchen is really a good place for dyeing: it is easy to clean and has good lighting, running water, and a stove. If they are not allowed to stand long, most dyestuffs can be washed off kitchen surfaces. A little household bleach does wonders on pots and counter tops. Look out for rougher surfaces, though, like elderly linoleum and wood: those are better protected by thick newspaper layers. There is no reason for a lot of mess, however; organize matters thoughtfully and there will be fewer spills. If you know you are incorrigibly messy, get a friend without that problem to share dyeing with you.

If you were going to dye only once or twice, it wouldn't much matter how you organized your dyes, but if you want to dye more often or if you are going to experiment with mixing colors, organize your dyes so these activities will be easy.

Dyes come to you, usually, as dry powders. (Some household dyes come already dissolved in liquids nowadays.) They are more convenient to use, to measure, and to manage if you first dissolve them in water and use that "stock solution" as your dye. Dyes keep just as well in this liquid form as in a powder. You'll need containers to store the stock solutions in. Soft-drink bottles with screw-on tops or plastic squeeze bottles make good ones. Containers that cannot be closed or metal ones that the dyes might react with won't do. Be sure to label the containers conspicuously and store them separately from food items.

It is only the amount of dye chemical, and not the amount of water in the dyebath that affects how strongly colored the yarns become. (The amount of water can affect the *rate* of dyeing: in a large amount of water the molecules of dye have to wander farther to get to the yarn, and dyeing proceeds more slowly.) Every dye packet tells you what weight of cloth or yarn it will dye to full color. Mix the amount of dye predicted to dye one pound (16 weight ounces) of fabric in one pint (16 volume ounces) of water to make your stock solutions. Then whenever you wish to dye one ounce (weight) of wool to a strong color, you will add one ounce (volume) of dye to the water in your dyepot. That dye can be of any color made by mixing the stock solutions. To dye to paler colors, use only a small part of an ounce of dye.

How to do all that measuring? Volume is easy: all kitchens have measuring cups and spoons.

Remember that 16 ounces (weight) equals 1 pound, while 16 ounces (volume) equals 1 pint. "A pint's a pound the world around" is an old rhyme that refers to a pint of water. Notice the distinction between volumetric and weight measure though: a pint of wool is no pound!

More volume measures

16 ounces =	1 pint
8 ounces =	1 cup
1 ounce =	2 tablespoons
3 teaspoons =	1 tablespoon
1 teaspoon =	100 drops

You can estimate the weight of wool by eye, by using a postage scale, or by making the simple scale described in the Appendix on Tools, to measure the yarns.

Weighing yarn.

One ounce of wool makes a ball about this big.

Mixing the Dye Solutions

Materials You Will Need

Dye powders
Storage bottles: Screw-top soda bottles or plastic squeeze jars or old jam
    jars.
Measuring cup
Hot water
A funnel or a steady hand
Bowl or pot: Of glass, enamel or stainless steel, to mix solutions in.
Stirrers: Stainless steel or plastic spoons, pencils, or throwaway sticks.
Paper, pencil, and labels
Cleanser, bleach, sponges

To mix these solutions, use kitchen utensils that you feel sure you can
really clean: enamel, stainless steel, smooth ceramic, or glass. Aluminum
pots may react chemically with dyes, so avoid them.

Put the dye powder in your mixing pot, add a few drops of water to
dampen all the powder, and mix until all lumps are gone. Then add the
right amount of very hot water—almost boiling hot—stirring all the while.
It is just like making cocoa. Use one pint of water with the amount of dye
powder predicted to dye a pound of goods. Transfer the mixed dyes into
the storage bottles and label them. These are your stock solutions of dye,
ready for use whenever you wish. They keep splendidly in this form.

Dyeing Yarns

Now you are ready to dye your yarns. Read the instructions that came with
your dye packets and make any changes you think are suitable in the
procedure that follows.

Materials You Will Need

Dyepots: Use stainless steel or enamel pots; or use glass jars in a big pan as
    a double boiler.
Yarn: Have it in loose skeins—see chapter 1 for making them. (Wool dyes
    so well that wool yarns are a good idea for your first experiments.)
Dye: In stock solutions.
Salt: (Either plain or iodized) To use if you want to speed up the dyeing
    process.
Sticks: (For moving yarn around in the hot dye solution) Pencils,
    chopsticks, the handles of stainless steel silverware, sticks from trees.
Measuring devices: Cups, spoons, and a tool for weighing if you wish.
A notebook, tags for labeling yarns and pots, and a pencil for marking
    (pencil marks won't dissolve in the solutions).
Rubber gloves
An apron
Bowls, sponges
Household bleach, detergent
Paper towels, newspaper

*Two ways to organize the simmering of
batches of yarn and dye. In the first, the
yarns and dye are heated in a pot. There
is plenty of room for the yarn and
stirring is easy. In the other the yarns
and their colors are in jars which in turn
are heated by a water bath, as in a
double boiler. It is possible to use a
really large pot, like a roasting pan, for
this. While it is harder to keep the yarns
stirred, it becomes easy to dye many
colors at one dyeing session. The "pot"
method gives the more even dyeing,
while the "double-boiler" method dyes
more yarn at one time.*

Gauge the weight of yarn you are dyeing. Now make the color you have in mind. Intermix your stock solutions, aiming to make about an ounce of dye for each ounce of wool you want strongly colored. If you have more dye than you need by the time the color is right, reserve the extra. You might use it to make a related color after you see how the first one comes out. The stock solutions appear very dark. You can get a notion of their true color if you mix a drop of them into a glass of water.

Untwist the skeins, making sure the yarns are loose. Wet the yarn before it goes into the dyebath, unless you want the yarn to be strongly mottled. The wet skeins can wait in a bowl of water until it is time for each one to be dyed. A few drops of liquid dishwashing detergent added to this soak will act as a "wetting agent," helping the water to get at all surfaces.

A Note about Wool and Shrinking:
Never change the temperature of wool suddenly: it's not high heat but quick changes of temperature that mat and shrink wool. Start with a cool dyebath, heating the solution and the wool together. When you take the wool out of a hot dyebath for rinsing, either let it cool in a bowl by itself, or start with very hot rinse water, cooling it gradually. Treat wet yarns gently, especially loosely spun ones: they can mat just from mechanical tangling.

Pick up wet skeins by their ties, not by the yarn itself. It is astonishing, but this treatment will keep them from tangling. When you finally wind them into balls, there will be no trouble.

Choose the dyebath method that you think will work best for you. Add cold water to your container: you need at least enough water to cover the wool. Use just enough to cover, if you want some variation in the resulting color. Use more water—up to thirty times the weight of the wool—if you want a more even dyeing. The amount of water will not affect how strong the color becomes; that depends only on time and how much dyestuff is there. Add the dye to the bath, and then add the wool. Heat it all slowly, bringing it to a simmer in ten to fifteen minutes.

Heat speeds all chemical reactions. Unless you want to wait many days for the dyeing to take place, simmer the yarns in their bath. Add salt to the solution if you want as much dye as possible to come out on the yarns. Use about as much salt as there was dye powder to begin with, although more won't do any harm.

Stir the contents of the dye pot every few minutes—but do it gently. One way is to lift the yarns out by their skein-ties and lower them again. That way, you can see the color developing on the yarns as well. When you color yarns yourself, you can dye evenly or you can let the color become mottled, varying just a little here and there. It can add a liveliness to your colors to have such variation from place to place. Less water, faster dyeing, less stirring, and bunched yarn all contribute to this rich effect. The liveliness of color obtained in this way can be very interesting in woven cloth.

When the color looks right, the dyeing is finished. (Remember colors look darker when they're wet.) Rinse out the extra dye, then squeeze the skein, removing what water you can without wringing or twisting. Hang your skein by its looped tie where it can drip.

Yarns dyed with onion skin.

You don't have to keep any result you don't like. You can overdye the yarn, dyeing a second time in another color, or you can remove the offending color by using the color remover sold by the makers of household dyes, and then start over. If you have dyed yarns a color you especially like, make small changes in that color and use those related colors for dye batches as well or dye some yarns in a more dilute bath of the same color. Such variations on a color theme are lovely to weave with. You can dye many skeins many colors in one session of dyeing. Often the colors you make early in a session give you ideas for other colors later. Have more skeins on hand than you have made plans for.

When you have done enough, clean up! Dye and food don't mix. Wash all pots well; wash the sink well. Household bleach and cleanser will get things truly clean again.

Dyeing with a Plant Stuff

Dyeing with material from plants is a richly rewarding experience, but not a simple one. There are difficult requirements that must be met. You must learn the best time to gather each plant; usually you must add special chemical substances to your dyebath to help the color blossom onto the yarn; often the plant you want grows only in a distant exotic place, or you would endanger a plant's future generations by picking present individuals now.

Sometimes all the problems fade away. Dyeing with the crisp, golden outer skin of the ordinary onion is a lovely way to avoid all those difficulties. In any season, onion skins are easy to come by, either by saving them at home, or by searching out the scraps at the bottom of your grocer's onion bin. The skins are easy to use, requiring no additive but water, and make a lovely color.

You will need a lot of onion skin, about half as much onion skin as wool, measured by the rough bulk measure of handfuls. Put the wool and the onion skin in the dyepot; add enough cool water to cover all and bring the pot to a simmer. Lift up the skein occasionally, watching the color develop. It will become a warm terra cotta brown in about an hour. The wool will not get darker than that if it is dyed longer, but you can try adding a second skein when the first one is removed. It will only become a pale variant on the first, but will still be a pleasant warm buff. Rinse the skeins and hang to dry.

If the process pleases you, you may want to explore that older, rewarding world of dyes and have the experience of gleaning your plants, coming to know them and their sunny days, releasing their colors onto your yarns. You can weave goldenrod and sumac, onion and walnut into your cloth. The books listed in the bibliography in the Appendix will get you started. When you gather plant materials, please pick them thoughtfully, conserving the plants for other years and other weavers.

Keep a record of the colors you have made. Jot down amounts as you work and later transfer that information to cards, attaching a yarn sample, or to a running notebook that keeps all the information together. This sort of record can become very beautiful and would be worth making for that reason alone. Not only does it allow you to repeat a color you once made—more or less—but it gives you a series of colors to study and think about. Add samples here, too, of yarns you buy and swatches of colors you are considering.

Dilutions

A set of yarns of the same color, but graded in intensity from very strong to very pale, are interesting to weave with and very easy to dye. To make such a set, start with six to eight skeins of yarn equal in length. Decide how much dye is needed to develop a strong color on one skein. Prepare about *three* times as much stock solution of dye as that, mixing to make the color you want. Put this dye in a measuring cup, add enough water to fill the cup, and use *half* of that solution in the dyebath for the first skein. Dilute the other half of the solution, still in the measuring cup, by refilling it with water; the solution is now half as strong. Use half of this solution in the second dyebath for the second skein.

Proceed thus for the other skeins, adding a half-cup of water to refill the dyecup and then using a half-cup of this diluted dye for the next skein. Throw out the final half-cup of solution after you've made your palest dyebath. How many times can you dilute and still have some color left?

Leave the yarns in their dyebaths for roughly equal lengths of time, to guarantee that the color series has smooth gradations. Although each color is only half as strong as the preceding one, they finally appear as equal steps, revealing something about the way our eyes work.

Space-Dyeing

Using different yarns of differing colors is not the only way to produce a weaving of many colors. A single strand can be dyed with many colors, and that yarn can be woven to make a new and different kind of color geometry in your web. The plan is to make a skein of wool with different colors at different parts of the skein, overlapping a little where the colors meet.

Dye the skein while keeping most of it out of the dye bath: only part of the skein becomes colored at one time. Dye as much or as little of the distance around the skein as you wish with each color. Rinse the yarn before moving on to the next color. Work your way around the skein until all is dyed. When you weave with yarn dyed like this, the colors repeat at a distance equal to the length of your skein. If you wish, you can plan ahead what length of skein will give you a desired effect. Or just play around when you dye such a yarn, using any skein that is handy, and explore afterward how to weave with it.

Yarns dyed in a dilution series.

Part of a skein being dyed.

Space-dyed yarns. Do you remember yarn like this from your childhood? Had you figured out how it was made?

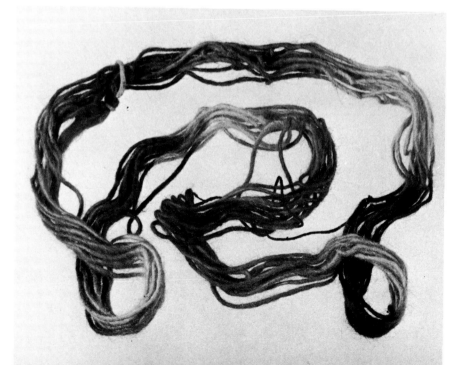

Tie-Dyeing

Another way of organizing the color on yarns is to tie-dye them. If a constriction is made in a bundle of yarns, and the yarns are then dyed, no dye can get at the squeezed section. Afterward those sections appear in the original color, contrasting to the dyed parts. Any firm string, wound around the yarns you plan to dye, will do this. Rubber bands work well, too. The blocked-off portion can be narrow—a few turns of string—or wide, blocking off the dye for inches. Once the dyeing is done, the ties can be taken off, or more ties can be added and the yarn dyed another color.

If a yarn so dyed is used randomly in a weaving, a flecked, random texture results. If the yarns are used in any way that preserves the original relationships of the parallel strands, striped areas of the original yarn color appear in the finished product. Often, both tie-dyed and solidly colored yarns are combined in a single weaving.

In some cultures yarns are prepared most elaborately in this technique and then are woven in a simple, straightforward manner. You can see a piece of this sort being woven in the photos on page 79. The Indonesian word for this technique is "ikat"; it is now often referred to thus. In other places around the world the patterns are more simply made and might suggest possibilities for you to adapt to your own use. The photos on this and page 18 are all blue and white textiles, with indigo as the dyestuff.

Two skeins of yarn, one dyed only, the other tied, dyed, and partially unwrapped. The skeins were made long enough to act as lengthwise yarns for a band before they were dyed. The striped piece was woven from these yarns plus the addition of a few darker ones for the narrow stripes

Stripes from Guatemala, with an elaborately ikat-dyed section of two figures. The yarns were subdivided into small bundles for this, each tied at the appropriate places.

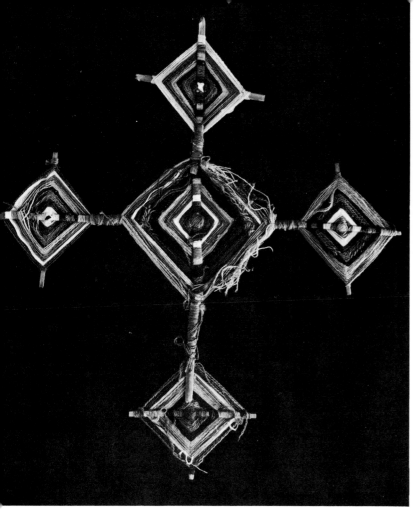

A very old god's eye, five-fold in
structure, from Peru. (The Peabody
Museum of Archaeology and Ethnology.
Photograph by Hillel Burger)

An extraordinary ancient wrapped tree
from Peru. Its leaves and the strange
figures perched in its branches are
woven. (The Denver Art Museum)

A god's eye made by a beginner
exploring the properties of hand-dyed
yarns. See others in the color section.

3. Spiders' Games: Less than Weaving

No one comes as a novice to any complicated human activity and is able immediately to produce with mature skill. Knowing this tells us that we did not come, as people in the past, to the bewildering array and diversity of what we now can weave without beginnings and an evolution of skills. One of the ways to explore the world is to play in it, as kittens and children do. Weavers have always made playful structures of their yarns—sometimes as exercises for young beginners, sometimes in joyful exuberance, sometimes just because the yarn was there and the fingers were idle. "Playing with threads makes no cloth, but playing with threads makes weavers."

Among such "games" have been swinging tassels, god's eyes like small banners, string figures, even the braids that kept the hair of weavers in order. You will find these arrayed here for you to learn, or to remind you of them and of how they are made. While everything in this chapter is easy to make, each technique has been valued and passed on by generations of workers with yarn. We commend all of them to you, along with others of your own invention, both for the fun and for the learning. Playing these weavers' games provides subtle lessons about tension and bulk, structure and management, permanence, texture, form, and more. Gaining the skills learned by making them is a happy preparation for weaving cloth.

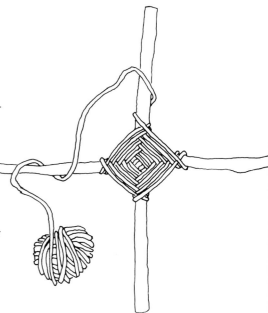

Winding a god's eye. The yarn winds around each cross-piece in turn. In this case, it goes over each cross-piece as it comes to it.

Windings, Wrappings, Bundles

God's eyes are little structures made by "almost-weaving" yarn around a pair of sticks. Most have come from the new world. They are still made in Mexico; long ago they were made in Peru, where the dry climate has preserved many articles made of fibers. What their original use or meaning was, no one knows. They were traditionally made of more than one color, an example you can follow if you wish.

In their simplest form, god's eyes are two sticks crossed, then wound about with yarns. They can be made in many different ways: use your ingenuity. You can vary the direction of turning or experiment with the color and texture of yarn. Try looking for the sticks in the woods or a vacant lot. You could begin with a branching twig and build your winding on those branches, developing a form in three dimensions, no longer flat. Finish off the yarns in any way that pleases you: a touch of white glue is sometimes better than knots.

Don't underestimate what you will learn from such a simple task. It is a way of building up a surface of yarns, similar to one of cloth, but without the under/over interlacement of weaving. How does the effect change when you lay the yarns closer or farther apart? What tension is enough and not too much? What effects can be made with a variety of colors?

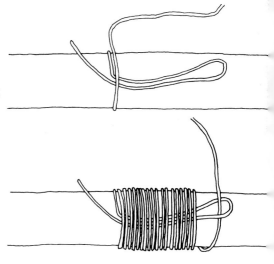

A stick or a rope is a good thing to use as the base for a first wrapping. There are many ways to finish loose ends: sew them under the wrapping, or glue them down. A particularly elegant method is used by sailors. Lay the start of your yarn down as a loop, over which you will wind. At the other end of the winding, slip the yarn end through that loop. Pull on the beginning end to draw the loop under the windings. Cut the ends off close to the wrap.

There are other things many ancient people made, close in spirit to these eyes of god: in some the yarns are wrapped around something: perhaps you have seen arrows whose shafts are wound carefully with striped patterns of colored yarns? A contemporary place to see the same effect is on fishing poles, holding the metal ferrules that guide the fishing line. Often these appear striped because they are wound of space-dyed thread. In other cases, yarn is wrapped around a bundle containing more yarns, producing a tassel. Find your own uses for these simple and handsome wrapping techniques.

This bundle of reeds wrapped with many different striped patterns was found by archaeologists in the grave of a Peruvian weaver. The purpose these decorated sticks had for their maker is no longer understood. (The Peabody Museum of Archaeology and Ethnology. Photograph by Hillel Burger)

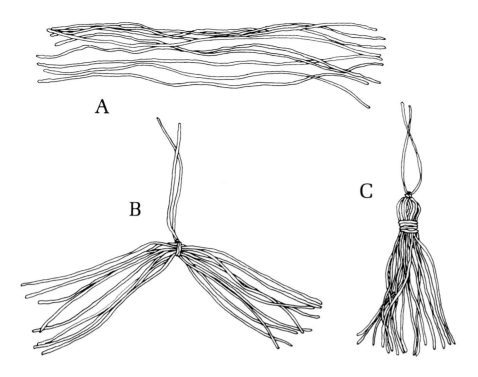

Tassels are made by wrapping around a bundle of yarns. To make such a structure, choose some yarns, all the same, or different in color and texture. A. Make a bundle twice as long and half as fat as you want the tassel to be. B. Tie the middle together. C. Fold the tassel in half and wrap it near the first tie.

A decorative ball from Japan wrapped in a manner reminiscent of a god's eye and finished with tassels.

A tasselled bag with braided handle made in Bolivia in this century. The tassels have been sewn on the finished bag. They appear to have been tie-dyed after they were formed. (The Peabody Museum of Archaeology and Ethnology. Photograph by Hillel Burger)

Rope Twining

Ropes—thick strands built up of many individual yarns—can be made by simple but elegant methods. Those ropes might be used as sashes or hair ties, or be added to bags as closures, edgings, and handles. Although ropes are made easily and quickly, the method is so appealing and the results so pleasant that suddenly you may find no yarns are left in the house. This is a good process to share with young children.

There are several ways to make rope; here is one way. You'll need a friend, a cup hook, a carpenter's "egg-beater" drill, as the figure shows, and several strands of yarn, all of one kind or mixed. Make a yarn bundle about two and a half times as long and half as thick as the rope you have in mind. Use the cup hook as though it were a drill bit, its threaded end in the drill: that makes a hook that turns round and round as you turn the drill.

Tie one end of your yarn bundle to something sturdy, like a doorknob and attach the other end to the cup hook. Pull the yarns taut and turn the drill. You will see the twist you are creating run down the yarn. Put in many twists, until the bundle of yarns seems very tight. Just how much twist is enough is hard to say, but a little experimentation will quickly show you what effects are possible.

When the bundle of yarns has been twisted, fold the yarn length in half. Have your friend hold the yarn bundle at the halfway point while you swing the end you are holding around to join the end at the doorknob. Pull on the yarn ends as you do this, to keep the bundles from bunching and curling. You no longer need the drill and hook or the doorknob, so slip the yarn ends off those and hold the doubled yarn with moderate tension between yourself and your friend.

Your friend should let go of the bundle slowly, working up the rope a few inches at a time, placing hand over hand. The rope will twist into being as each section is released. If too much is freed at once, it may bunch up: but pulling and sliding the rope through the fingers will usually fix that. If for any reason you don't like the product, the yarn bundle can be opened up and retwisted from the beginning. The amount of twist in the finished rope depends on how many turns were put in originally: adjust that to please yourself. The folded end of the rope won't untwist, but the other end would if you let it. You might tie an overhand knot in that end, and ravel out the individual yarns to make a tassel.

You can also twist yarns for rope using a household electric drill. This way is noisy, but exciting.

Twisting a rope using an egg-beater drill, a cup hook, and a doorknob. The rope being made here is unusually short.

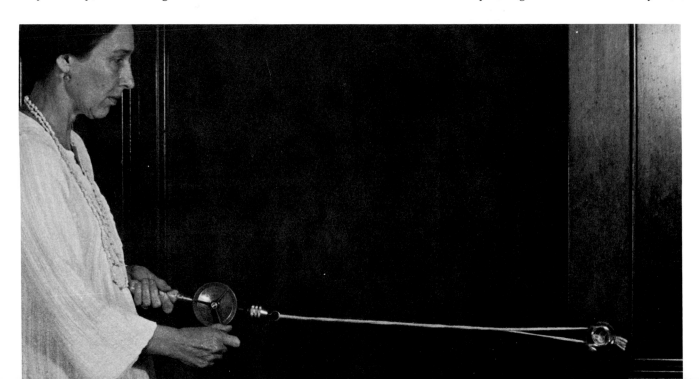

The rope begins to form as the hands "walk" up the twisted and doubled yarn bundles.

A short length of rope, twisted from woolen yarn.

If you have no drills, here is another way. You'll need an empty thread spool and a pencil. Prepare your yarns as before and tie one end to a secure place. Poke the other end through the hole in the spool, and tie the yarn ends together with an overhand knot. Slide the pencil in between the knot and the spool. Hold the spool and pull on it to tighten the yarn; the pencil will be pulled across the flat end of the spool. Twist the pencil as though it were a propeller: the twist will travel up the yarn. When the yarn is twisted enough, proceed by folding the yarn length in half as in the hand-drill method, then walking the twist up the rope with your fingers.

Variations

A single strand of yarn instead of a bundle will produce a two-ply yarn.

After making a rope by twisting and doubling, try retwisting and redoubling that rope.

Does the direction of twist matter?

Try using many strands of one kind of yarn—enough so one twisting and folding bring it to the girth you had in mind.

Try many strands of various yarns, treated as one bundle for twisting and folding.

Try two kinds of yarn tied together in the middle where they will be folded.

Try several bundles of different yarns, each twisted separately, but with the same direction of twist, and then brought together as though you were folding them. With no fold, both ends of this rope will need a knot to secure the twist.

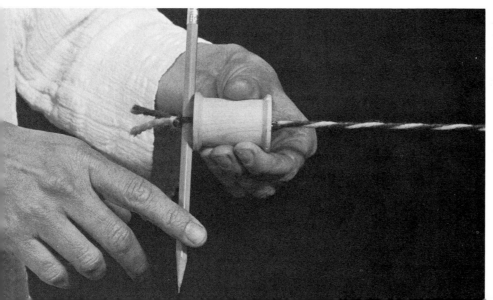

The "spool and pencil" method of rope twisting.

Braids, Plaits, and Pigtails

Quite different from rope in their looks, in their physical properties, and in the methods by which they are made are braids. They are rather like one-dimensional weavings, long and narrow, the yarns interlaced. They can be made with yarn used singly or in bunches, of a single color or many. Like ropes, they are easy to unmake if you don't like the result, so do experiment. Braids can be formed as functional or as whimsical articles, complete in themselves, or they can be used as details that finish other weavings.

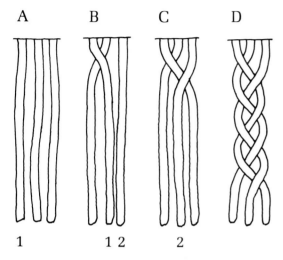

Three-strand braid:
A. Start with three strands.
B. Take the left outside strand, 1, put it between the other two strands.
C. Then take the right outside strand, 2, put it between the other two strands.
D. Continue, alternating from side to side, pulling up as tight as you wish.

Four-strand flat braid:
A. Start with four strands.
B. Cross center strands; 1 over 2.
C. Bring right strand to center; 3 over 1.
D. Bring left strand to center; 4 under 2, over 3.
E. Continue alternately in this way: 5 over 4 is next. It is possible to make flat braids of any number of strands greater than four in much the same way. Start by crossing two strands near the center of the set. This is often called "finger weaving" and can be made as wide as you can manage.

Three-strand braid

Four-strand flat braid

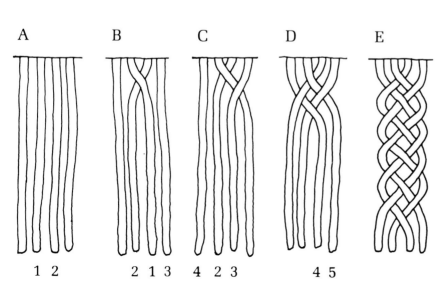

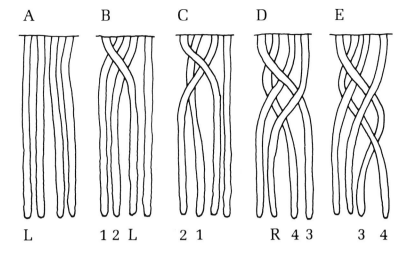

A B C D E

L   1 2 L   2 1   R 4 3   3 4

Four-strand round braid:
A. Start with four strands.
B. First side. Cross left outside strand
   over two strands.
C. Cross to left, strand 2 over 1.
D. Second side. Cross outside right
   strand over two strands.
E. Cross to right, strand 4 over 3.
Continue, alternating sides.

Four-strand round braids of two colors.
The final pattern depends upon the
order in which the colored strands are
laid out before starting to braid.

Your Hands Are a Loom

All around the world people play cat's cradle or other string games. These games are surely very old, passed down to us over generations from one person to another. They are too ephemeral to appear beneath the archaeologist's trowel, yet who can doubt that they are old as weaving and spinning?

The figure we share with you here as a sample of the craft came from the Caroline Islands in the Pacific, where it is called "Ten Men." You will need your hands and a piece of supple string, about 6 to 8 feet long, tied into a loop.

The diagrams show your two hands held up (thumbs nearest you) and the string. The finger you will need for the next move is darkened, and the place you will next pick up the string is marked by an "x."

Most people need to work through a string figure several times before it comes out well. Persevere: it really can be done.

The string figure called "Ten Men"

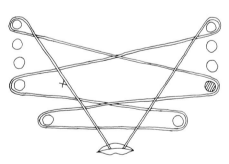

A. *Face palms toward each other, thumbs near you. Put string around back of little fingers and thumbs.*

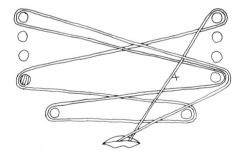

B. *Send right index finger across to pick up left palm string and return home. Unless it says otherwise, pick up the string by sending your finger under the string to be picked up, picking the string up from below.*

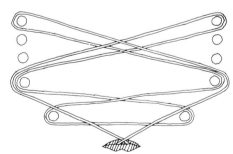

C. *Do the same operation with your left index finger.*

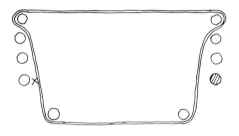

D. *Reach over the near strings and pick up the most distant string with your mouth. Draw it back home.*

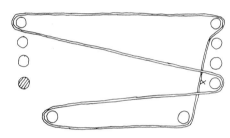

E. *Send your right index finger across and pick up left mouth string. Return home. This makes two loops on the right index finger. Have the new loop rest nearer the tip of the finger, with the old loop down lower. In these drawings, new loops are always shown outside older loops.*

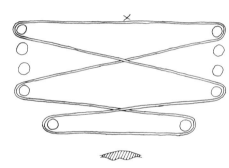

F. *Repeat for the other side.*

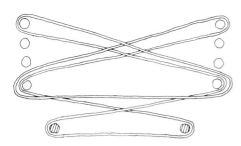

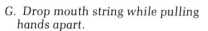

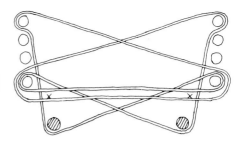

G. Drop mouth string while pulling hands apart.

H. Drop thumbs. Separate hands to take up slack, all the while keeping newer loops nearer tips of index fingers than older loops.

I. Send both thumbs under 1 2 3 4 threads. Pick up thread from little finger and return home under 1 2 3 4.

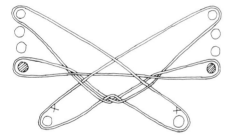

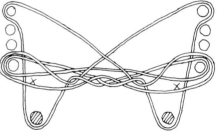

J. With tip of thumbs, pick up loop that perches near tip of index fingers. Return thumbs home, without dropping any loops.

You now have two loops on both thumbs and index fingers. Make sure all the newer loops are higher up on the fingers.

K. With teeth, pull out lower thumb loop, lift it around upper thumb loop and tip of thumb. Drop this loop on palm side of thumb. Do this for both thumbs.

L. Drop upper loop on index fingers, separating hands.

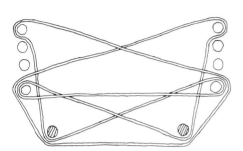

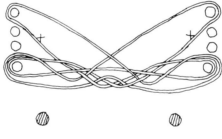

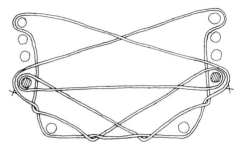

M. Transfer thumb strings to index fingers. Keep new loop near tip of index. There will be no strings left on thumbs.

N. Send thumbs below the index finger threads, pick up thread from little finger, and return back home. (This, and the next two steps, are much as you did before.)

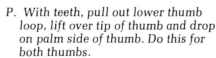

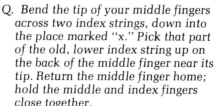

P. With teeth, pull out lower thumb loop, lift over tip of thumb and drop on palm side of thumb. Do this for both thumbs.

Q. Bend the tip of your middle fingers across two index strings, down into the place marked "x." Pick that part of the old, lower index string up on the back of the middle finger near its tip. Return the middle finger home; hold the middle and index fingers close together.

O. With tip of thumb, pick up loop nearest tip of index finger. Be sure the older thumb and index loops remain lower down on those fingers.

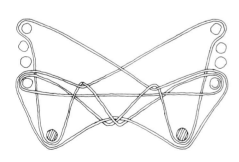

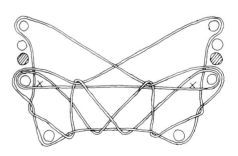

You are now ready to display the figure. Gently drop your little finger strings, extend your thumbs and pull your hands apart, as in the drawing of "Ten Men." If you turn your palms away from you as you do this, the figure has a dramatic quality: it is easy to understand why they so often occur in the context of storytelling.

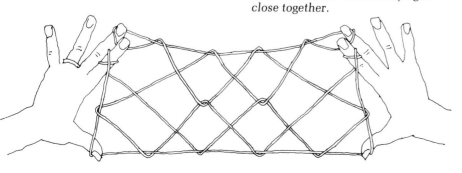

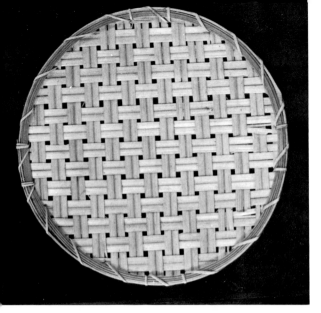

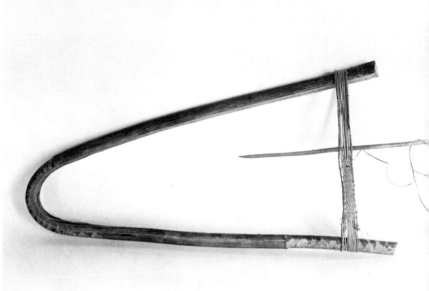

The coarse elements used in many baskets boldly show the structure of their weave: the plain-weave interlacement of this flat Japanese tray can be clearly seen. The materials used to make baskets are usually less flexible than those used for cloth, and the forms are manipulated without a loom to hold them. Basketry forms were made and used long before spun yarns were ever woven into supple cloth.

From the Solomon Islands in the Southeast Pacific, a "least" loom, for weaving a short strip. The bent bow holds the warp strands under tension, the needle carrying the weft strand sews over-and-under, through the warps, row after row. (The Ethnographic Museum, Basel)

The weaver's fingers manipulate the warp threads of this narrow weaving from Indonesia, finding a complex path through them so the weft will display the developing flowerlike pattern. (Photograph by Monni Adams)

Three Ways To Weave

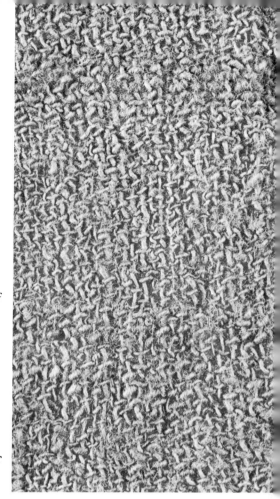

All weaving involves the interlacement of fibers and results in a cloth that seems much more than the sum of its strands. The simplest, the most typical interlacement is of single elements that cross alternately over and under each other. This is known as "plain weave." Our world is full of examples of plain weave: handkerchiefs, sheets, in fact most of the weaving ever made. Making that cloth is a two-step process: first, one set of fibers is aligned in parallel array and held fixed; second, the other set of fibers is worked through, over and under, alternating threads, alternating rows, locking separate strands into the textile web.

The first set of yarns—the warps—stretched, parallel, passive, are held by the loom: that structure, any structure, holding yarns ready for the weaving. The second set, the active weft yarns, grow row by row upon the framework of the warp yarns, worked through them by fingers, needles, sticks and loops of string, or by the extraordinary, automatic mechanisms of modern times.

The properties of woven cloth are many; it can be thick or gossamer, supple or stiff, smooth or rough or fuzzy. Cloth can keep you warm, dry, or unbitten; it can decorate you; it can contain your belongings, harness beasts, flap in breezes, or present stories in pictures. Both the material fibers with which you weave and the structure you impose upon them affect these qualities. The first, and in many ways the most powerful, of the structural variations in cloth is caused by the spacing of warp and weft yarns relative to each other.

If the distance between the warp threads is more or less the same as that between the wefts, and the plain-weave interlacement of over one, under one is followed, both sets of fibers show in the finished cloth. Such cloth can be described as having the commonest, the most ordinary of all possible weaves, so pervasive it has no clearly defined name. Weavers call it "balanced plain weave" or "tabby."

But that spacing need not be the same in both directions. Either the warp or the weft yarns can be spaced more and more closely, coming to dominate and finally to cover entirely the other set of yarns. If it is the warp yarns that you see in the finished cloth, then the cloth is "warp-faced"; if the weft yarns show, it is "weft-faced."

These changes modify the properties of the cloth. When you make long, narrow weavings of warp-faced weaves, with the warps going in the long direction, the cloth is very strong along its length and makes good belts, straps, and ties. If you look at the body of a cloth of balanced plain weave, and not at its smooth-woven edges, it is not obvious which were the warps and which the weft yarns. The properties of the cloth are not markedly different in different directions. Finally, weft-faced weave yields a cloth where only the actively woven yarns show in the final fabric. Since these are, step by step, row by row, under the control of the weaver, it is a way of weaving that permits decisions and changes on the part of the weaver even as the cloth is being woven. Tapestry weaves and many pattern weaves are weft-faced.

Balanced plain weave cloths from two ancient traditions, with their yarns crossing alternately over and under, the relative spacing the same for warp and weft. The paler linen is from Coptic Egypt, the darker wool from pre–Columbian Peru. Cloth similar to these is being woven every day, both by hand and by machine.

The following chapters demonstrate three ways to weave cloths like this. You could think of these three chapters as a journey back through time, for each one shows you a method older than the one before. You will be introduced first to a modern, clever way to use a piece of cardboard as your loom to make a weft-faced bag; then to methods used in medieval Europe for weaving narrow warp-faced bands; and finally to our versions of one of the most ancient and general ways to weave pieces of cloth. This last way has been invented at various times by all peoples who wove and is still in use all over the world today. The first two methods produce special kinds of cloth. The third method is broadly versatile and will allow you to move on in directions of your own choosing. The methods have been arranged as they are because the skills and understandings they require of you build in complexity: each technique supposes that you have understood the previous one. They have also been chosen because each of them allows you to make a beautiful and interesting cloth.

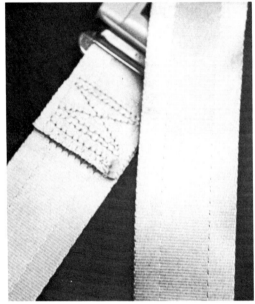

Be looking for examples of variations in the relative spacing of warp and weft yarns in everyday life. A handkerchief is woven in balanced plain weave. Automobile seatbelts are of a complex warp-faced weave. Some terrycloth towels have weft-faced borders; in our example the weft yarn passes over several warp threads at a time, no longer plain weave, but a weft-faced twill (see chapter 9).

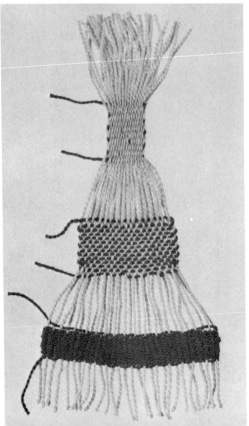

A sampler of weaves. All three woven areas here are plain weave: the interlacement is over one, under one. In the top area, only the lengthwise warp threads are showing: there the cloth is warp-faced. The center area, showing both pale warps and dark wefts, is balanced; the bottom area is weft-faced. If you imagined weaving in those areas where the warps are now empty, that cloth would gradually shift from being warp-faced to becoming balanced and then weft-faced. Such in-between weaves are referred to as "predominantly warp- or weft-faced."

4. Weft-faced Weaving: Making a Bag

Weavings in which the weft yarns predominate in the design are made all over the world. The technique is used especially when the weaver wants great personal freedom in shaping the product, when each article is to be unique. Much contemporary weaving made for nonutilitarian uses by textile artists meets that criterion, and indeed many modern weavers employ weft-faced weaves in their work. Weft-faced textiles are also used within traditional cultures. Navaho weavers, who make every blanket or rug different, are an example.

In all weaving the warp yarns form the passive scaffolding upon which the active weft yarns are woven. In weft-faced weaving, only the active weft elements show on the surface of the finished cloth. Since each weft yarn need not be chosen until the moment it is woven into the textile, the weaver is free to base decisions of what to do next upon what the cloth looks like so far. All effects do not have to be planned out beforehand: the plan can grow as the cloth does, row after row. There is often much spontaneity to weft-faced weaving for just this reason.

The weaving we will be doing in this chapter is to be a weft-faced bag, woven on a specialized bag-loom into the enclosed shape of a container. It will be woven complete, needing no seams. Although good-sized bags can be made this way, your first weaving should be a small object, requiring the very least of equipment and material.

Small weft-faced bags woven by beginners.

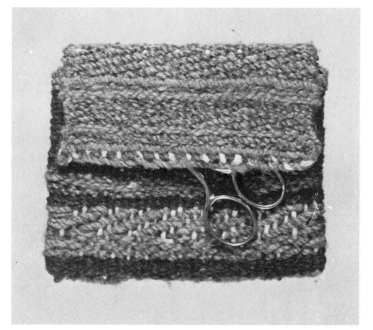

Making a Bag on a Cardboard Loom

Materials You Will Need

A piece of moderately stiff cardboard: This can be the back of a pad of
paper, stiff oaktag, or chipboard. (Chipboard can be bought
inexpensively at art stores.) Make the cardboard the size you want for
your finished bag. We have seen bags larger than 9 by 12 inches, but
suggest 4 by 6 inches or smaller for a first try. A 3 by 4 inch bag could
hold change or buttons, a little shell or pebble collection, or a favorite
necklace. A glasses case or a chocolate-bar bag could be 3 by 7 inches.

A long needle with a big eye: These are most useful if they are longer than
the width of your bag. The longest ones—8 to 20 inches—are called
baling needles. You can make suitable needles for yourself from coat
hangers or umbrella ribs (see the Appendix on Tools) or you can use a
shorter needle with a big eye.

Warp yarn: For the warp, the supporting thread, use either a strong wool,
preferably plied, or a smooth cotton yarn. Crocheting cotton from the
dime store would work well. The warp yarn can be manipulated either
to be entirely invisible, or it can show at the bag's opening. In that case
you may prefer a wool yarn that goes well with your wefts.

Weft yarn: For the weft, the weaving thread, you'll want a collection of
odds and ends whose colors together give you pleasure. The more
texture the better: you may even want to twist some threads around each
other before you weave with them.

Pencil, ruler, scissors, comb

1. *Beginning to warp the loom.*

Preparing the Warp

Cut the cardboard to the size you wish. The bag will be woven right over
this and will be the size and shape of the cardboard. Decide which edge
you wish to be the open edge in the finished bag.

Make a series of marks for slots along that edge, making the marks about
¼ inch apart. If possible, have the marks at the corners closer than ¼ inch
to the corners. With scissors, cut into the cardboard just a bit at each mark:
a ⅛-inch bite is plenty. This is your loom, which you now can begin to
warp.

To begin warping the loom, place the yarn in the first notch, as you see
in Figure 1. It should wedge there tightly. Let the free end hang out 6
inches or so.

Bring the warp thread down over one side of the cardboard, around the
bottom, and up the other side (fig. 2). Wedge the thread into the same
notch as before. Bring it back through the second notch. Tighten the thread
both where it goes around the bottom of the cardboard and where it
crosses from notch to notch, so that it lies straight, with no loose loops.

Bring the thread around the bottom of the cardboard, up into notch two
and immediately back through notch three (fig. 3). Tighten as before.
Continue in this manner, *never going over the top edge of the bag loom
with your yarn*, except to come right back through the next notch. When
you have done it correctly, it will look like Figure 4.

You will have ended up at the top, with an even number of warps
around the loom—as many on one side as on the other. You need an odd
number of threads for the in-and-out of the weaving to work, so cut an
extra notch at the bottom corner and have your warp thread end there (fig.
5). Break off the warp with a few inches hanging free. You are now ready
to weave.

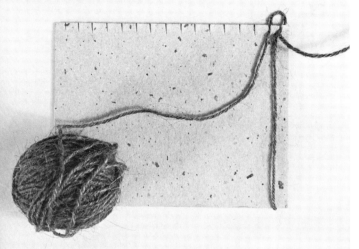

2. Coming back through the second notch. The cardboard has been turned over.

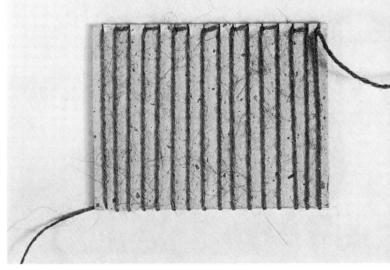

5. The warp in the final notch on the lower edge.

3. Warping the third notch.

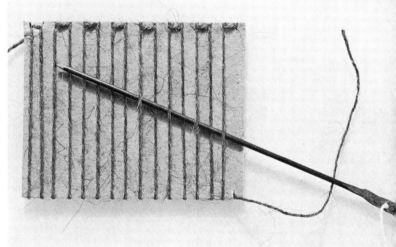

6. Starting to weave.

4. Warping is almost complete.

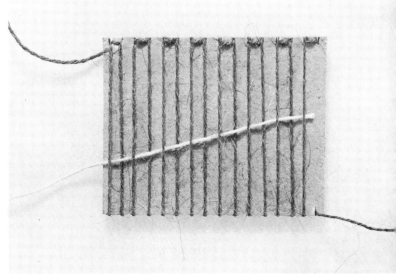

7. The first row of weaving.

Weaving the Bag

People who are new to weaving often have troubles with edges, where the weaving thread turns around and goes back the way it came. There will be no such trouble here: this weaving goes round and round and there are no side edges.

Weaving starts at the bottom of the bag-to-be. Choose the yarn that you want to weave there. Cut a piece of it as long as your outstretched arm can reach. Thread the needle with this yarn; "sew" it under one warp, over the next, and so on, across the first side of the bag (fig. 6).

Pull the yarn through until the far end just enters the weaving (fig. 7). With your fingers or a comb, push the weaving yarn—the weft—down as closely as you can to the bottom of the bag (fig. 8). This is called "beating" the yarn.

Look at the last warp thread through which you've just woven. Does the weft cross over or under it? When you turn the cardboard to weave across the other side of the bag, you'll need to start that row the opposite way: under if over, over if under! Weave the second side, and beat the weaving down there too.

As you return to the first side to begin the second round of weaving, you no longer need to remember how you finished the side before: you only need to do the opposite of what you did when last you went this way. Where the first pass of the old weft is over, go under, and vice versa (fig. 9).

Keep weaving round and round this way until the bottom stripe is as broad as you wish. If you run out of thread before this occurs, start a new thread. Weave the old thread until it is ended. When you are almost at the end of a thread, it becomes too short for the beginning of the needle to enter the warps. Turn the needle around and send it through backwards (fig. 10).

To start weaving with new thread, overlap the wefts about four or five warp threads. It doesn't matter where along a row that happens. Either break off or cut the ends of new wefts: cutting is often convenient, while broken ends are inconspicuous. Don't make knots; they always show or change the feel of the cloth (fig. 11).

Start a second color or texture of yarn in the same way. If it is easier for you to leave old ends dangling, that is all right, too. Overlap the old and new threads, as in Figure 12; cut off the loose ends later.

As your bag grows, keep thinking of the new possibilities for further development that it suggests to you. Remember, too, that you can make other bags to explore those ideas that come to you as you work.

When the weaving reaches the top of the cardboard and it becomes hard to enter any more weft, you have finished. Slip the warps at the top of your bag out of their notches and slide the bag down off its cardboard loom (fig. 13). You'll be surprised at its suppleness in your hands, now that it's free from tension. Darn the loose warp ends inconspicuously into the weave of the bag with an ordinary big-eyed needle. Look at what you have made. Consider it carefully. Should it have a closure or a handle? Is it complete?

Before you try a second weaving using this technique think about what things you could change. Can you plan a different sort of top edge? Is there a way for the sides to be different? How could you add a flap? Should the bag have a fringe on the bottom? Or different yarn spacing?

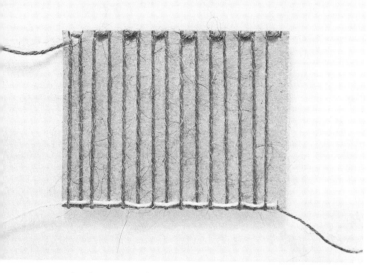

8. The first row of weaving, beaten down.

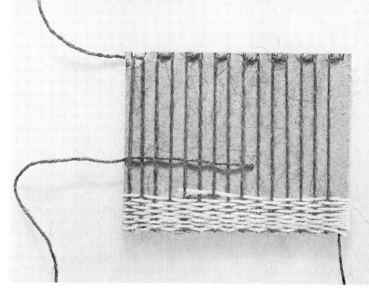

11. Starting a new weft yarn.

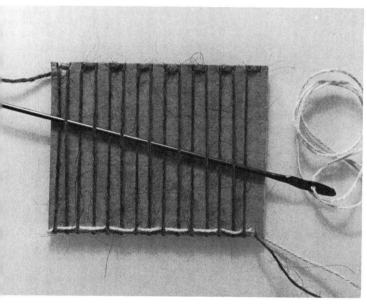

9. Beginning the second row of weaving.

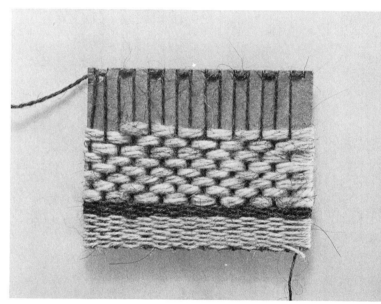

12. Three textures of yarn in one weaving.

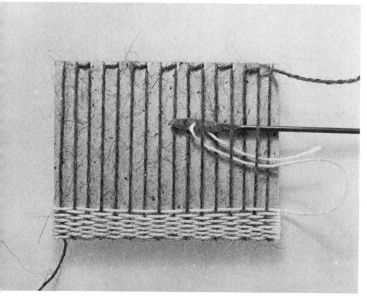

10. Weaving the very end of a thread, with the needle backward.

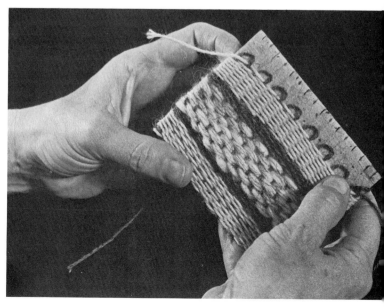

13. Removing the finished bag.

Finishes

Most bags are complete just as they are when slipped from their cardboard loom, but some want extra touches to become fnished. A bag can be held closed with a little zipper, or a loop-and-button, or a drawstring. If it were too open in its weave, it could be lined. It could have a handle made of braid or rope, or of a narrow band such as you will learn to make in the next chapter. It could be embellished with beads of seeds, fringe or tassel. There are no rules, and there is no limit to the possibilities. The photos on this page and page 41 in this chapter show some of these.

Perhaps the earliest artifacts men or women made, along with or even before hunting tools, were gathering tools. The first ones might have been made of folded leaves from large plants; soon they were made of plant fibers that were turned, twisted, or knotted. Their technological and material descendants—things to put things in—are baskets and woven bags.

Many bags woven within different folk traditions find their way into our world. Be looking for them hanging in shops and in museums, pictured in books, and being carried by people. Because their relatively small size permits complex weaves to be executed without too great a cost of time, they are often examples of showy patterned weaving. After a while, you will come to recognize where they were made.

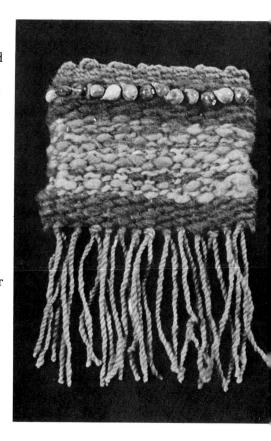

A simple striped bag from Mexico.
Chapters 7 and 8 have many suggestions
for weaving stripes.

More stripes, this time a child's small
carrying bag from present-day Peru.
(The Peabody Museum of Archaeology
and Ethnology. Photograph by Hillel
Burger)

Small brocade-woven bags from Mexico.

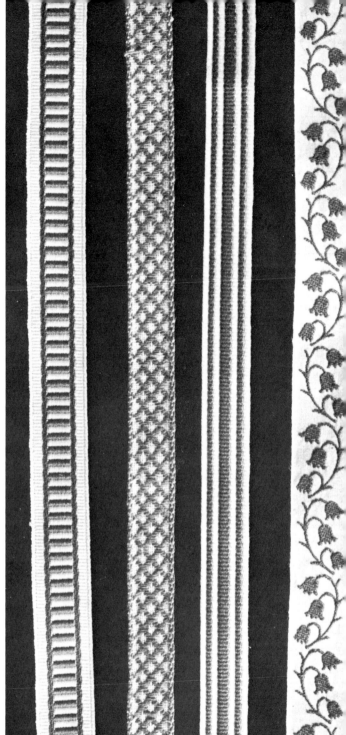

Four pretty ribbons, all woven by machine. Three of them are warp-faced.

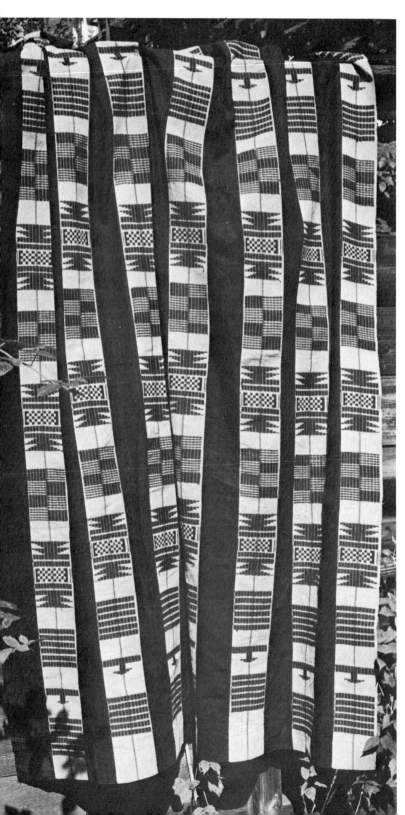

A large cloth made of fourteen narrow bands, each woven 4 inches wide, then sewn to each other. This was made in Nigeria, where such cloths are used for the wrapped skirts that women wear, or are sewn into the great loose robes worn by men.

5. Warp-faced Weaving: Making a Narrow Band

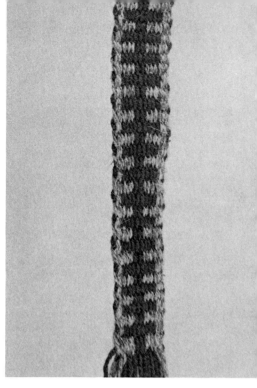

All-wool and a yard wide is not the only way that cloth is made. Cloth is also woven in narrow strips, ranging from very narrow indeed to bands a few inches wide. Such cloth is usually woven on a loom specifically designed for narrow weaving: The span of a weaver's hand controls the maximum width of the product. The photo of the narrow weaving from Indonesia in the Introduction to Part 2 (p. 38) shows such a loom.

Ribbons and belts, tape for tieing bundles, straps for harnesses and bags, and decorative edges on wider weavings are all examples of textiles deliberately woven in the shape of narrow bands. While these bands are most often used in their original narrow form, sometimes they are sewn together, becoming in this way wide enough to be the clothing, bedding, wrapping, or sheltering tent for the weaver—whatever is needed.

Although that is not the only way they can be woven, the majority of narrow weavings are warp-faced or predominantly warp-faced. This not only makes them strong in the long direction; it makes them easier to weave, for narrow weavings tend to become warp-faced during the process of weaving unless the weaver takes care to prevent it. Since it is the warp yarn that shows in these weavings, their patterns depend on the warp yarns and must be understood and organized at the time those yarns are set up. That makes patterned band weavings more complicated to plan than were the bags woven on cardboard looms. Many kinds of patterning are traditional for strip weavings, from simple and straight-forward long stripes to elaborate geometric forms. Chapter 8 will put you in touch with those traditions.

The yard-wide cloth requires a heavy loom with many individual parts and great strength to hold up under the tension of many threads. Narrower weavings permit less machinery to be used, which is an advantage to beginning weavers as well. When the cloth is narrow, the weaver can be very close to the weaving. The hand can span the warp and the fingers can reach into and through the yarns. The number of warp yarns does not overwhelm, the tension needed to hold the warp in alignment is not too great. The loom can be simple.

Simple as they are, the looms you will use to weave bands have an ingenious mechanism that frees the weaver from sewing the weft over and under each warp. This mechanism—the "heddle"—creates a clear opening through the warp threads, dividing the alternate yarns into separate groups, allowing the weft thread to weave a whole row with a single unbroken motion. This magical opening, the "shed," and the heddle mechanism that exchanges one shed for the other, is one of the great ancient human inventions, as revolutionary as the later invention of the wheel. Once this process was developed, clothing and all other textiles could be made with extraordinary efficiency, and the world was changed in many ways. The availability of woven cloth freed people from their dependence on animal skins for clothing and bedding and made it possible to live in larger groups and in harsher climates. At the same time, the need to use numbers and understand their relationships in order to weave the cloth encouraged the growth of abstract skills.

A belt of warp-faced weave. This pattern, which is found again and again in different cultures, was made by the order in which the warp yarns were set up. Once the warps were organized, the weaving proceeded without special manipulations of any kind and the pattern appeared automatically.

Three small bands, handwoven in complex traditional Latvian weaves.

This chapter will acquaint you with two different band-looms. The first uses an old tool called a rigid heddle, which was probably invented in Northern Europe in early medieval times. Belts and bands are quickly and easily made with this tool. Its effectiveness was appreciated by weavers: its use spread quickly all over the world, while it continued to be popular in Scandinavia where many traditional patterns are still woven with rigid heddles.

The other band-loom we present in this chapter has a set of heddles made of a stick and some string. This is a Baltic version of a more general type of loom than the rigid heddle; it appears second because the technique is not as easily mastered. Both looms introduce you to the heddle and shed that open the way for the weft yarn to follow its complex paths, and both will lead you to experience the rhythm of weaving, the dance of hand and body turning linear thread into a web of fabric.

Rigid heddles have alternate slots and holes through which the warp yarns pass. Old ones were usually made of wood, bone, even ivory; modern ones, like those shown here, are made of wood, metal, or plastics. The old ones were often charmingly decorated; you might consider adding your own embellishment to a heddle you have bought.

This old rigid heddle was made by an Indian of the northern woodlands. Rigid heddles were not known in that part of the world before the European settlers came. The design of hearts and leaves on this heddle strongly suggests that a Scandinavian tradition was seen and used by the Indian weavers. (The Milwaukee Public Museum)

How To Weave a Band
with a Rigid Heddle Loom

Materials You Will Need

A rigid heddle: This can be made of wood, metal, or plastic. It should be light and small; it need not have more than twenty holes, which should not be too small for the yarns you will choose for warps; holes and slots should both be smooth to the touch. The heddle will be easier to use it if is not too wide—perhaps under 10 inches. Since not all weavers' supply shops carry small rigid heddles mail-order sources are listed in the Appendix on Tools.

Two pieces of strong string, each four feet long.

A big-eyed needle, or a hairpin: With this you can pull yarns through the holes in the heddle if necessary.

Yarn for the warp: For your first band weaving, use a plied yarn that holds up to scraping wear from the holes in the heddle. Test a doubtful candidate by scratching it several times with your fingernail; if it comes apart readily it will not make a satisfactory warp. Weavers' supply shops will offer good advice. If you choose a yarn that keeps breaking, consider that a lesson learned and save the yarn to be used as weft. Even for your first project you might use several colors of yarn.

A small shuttle: It could be as simple as a piece of stiff cardboard, 1½ by 5 inches.

Yarn for the weft. You will want to experiment with your first weft, so it's hard to predict precisely what you will need. The yarn need not be the same as your warp yarn—it could be thicker or thinner. Its color will show only at the edge of the weaving; it need not be especially strong or resistant to abrasion.

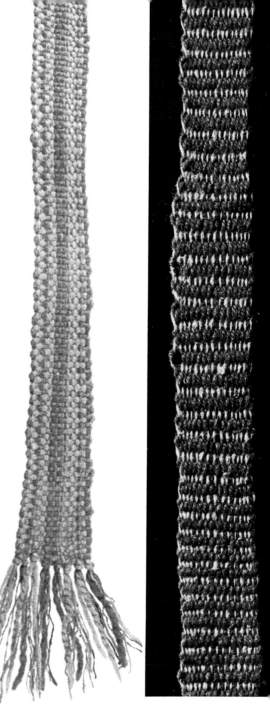

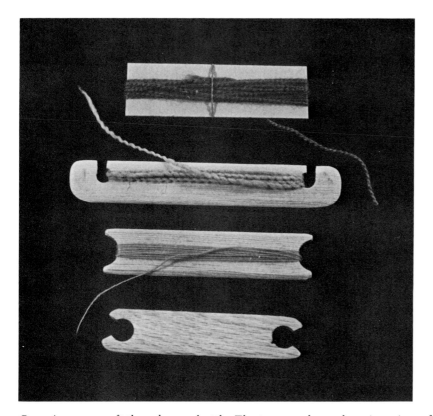

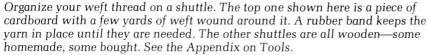

Organize your weft thread on a shuttle. The top one shown here is a piece of cardboard with a few yards of weft wound around it. A rubber band keeps the yarn in place until they are needed. The other shuttles are all wooden—some homemade, some bought. See the Appendix on Tools.

Planning

How long should the warp be? For your first project, a four-foot warp would make a short belt or sash; add another foot to allow you to weave experimentally at the beginning. After the first band, you will be able to manage longer warps and you will know how to judge the length you need.

How many warps should you use? At first, avoid too many strands; stay under forty. Fewer yarns will be easier to manage. Thicker yarns will make a wider band than an equal number of thin yarns. You can judge approximately what width a given number of warps will produce: the warps you use will be packed together in much the same way as the wefts were for the woven bags in the last chapter. Look at a bag you have woven to help you see how wide a given number of yarns would become when woven.

Another way to plan a band's width is to wind the yarn you are planning to use for the warp around a piece of cardboard, packing the yarns neatly and snugly next to each other, as in Figure 1. When this appears as wide as you wish your band to be, count the number of yarns and multiply that number by two. You need to double the number because at any given time in a warp-faced weaving half the yarns are on one face of the weaving, while half are on the other face.

How much weft yarn will you need? For your first weaving predictions are difficult. If you use the same yarn for weft and warp, then you will need less yarn for the weft in a warp-faced weaving. But if you decided to use those weft yarns doubled or even quadrupled, you would use much more yarn. It is usually safe to have the same number of yards put aside for warp and weft, providing you count the yards after doublings and such are made.

Preparing the Warp

For your first band, try making long stripes or a random arrangement of colored yarns. For stripes, place several warp threads of the same color next to each other. Make a rough chart of your planned arrangement.

Once you have planned the pattern, cut all the warp yarns to approximately the same length. There are many ways to measure. A simple way is to draw the yarn through your fingers, fold it at the correct length and draw the two threads along until you come back to the beginning; fold and repeat. Cut across the ends when you have folded enough strands.

Knot one end of the warp bundle together. Tie one of the pieces of strong string around the warps, next to the knot. The loose ends of the string should be a couple of feet long. Lay the warp bundle across a table, bend the string over the edge and tie it around a table leg. Sit across the table with the warp coming toward you, falling down over the edge near you (fig. 2).

From within the bundle of warps, find that color of thread which you wish to use at the edge of the band: pick it out from near the knot and draw it toward you, shaking it free of the rest of the warp. Thread this yarn through the heddle, through either a slot or a hole, where you figure the edge of the warp should come. The heddle will be a little easier to use later if you arrange your threading so the warps are approximately centered in the heddle. Perhaps the warp can be poked through by just folding the yarn; you may need a big-eyed needle, a hairpin, or a bent wire to help with fat yarns (fig. 3).

The second thread will go next to the first, through a hole if the first went through a slot, or vice versa.

Don't despair if it all seems very slow. By the time the warp is ready for weaving, you will have half-finished the project! After the yarns have been

1. A method for judging how many warps will make a certain width of band.

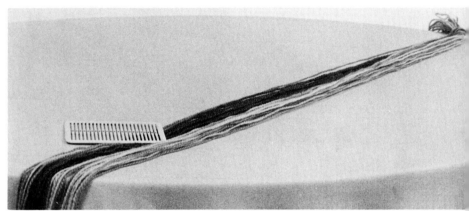

2. The warp tied to the table.

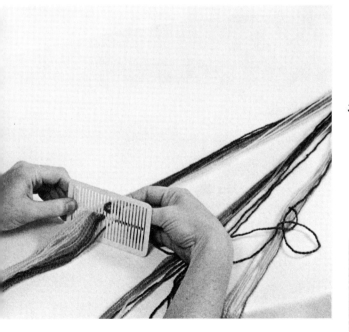

3. The warp half-threaded.

4. Combing the warp to even the tension.

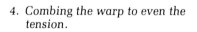

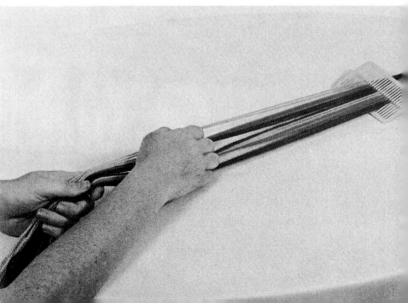

threaded through the heddle, inspect carefully to make sure they are in the order you had planned and that there are no gaps in slot or hole. Slide the heddle somewhat nearer to the knot at the far end of the warp and comb the warp through your fingers from the heddle to the free ends, as Figure 4 shows. This evens the tension on the yarns—an important matter for easy weaving. Stroke in this way until you are sure the yarns have very similar tensions, then knot the near end of the warp yarns the same way as the far end. Knot the second piece of strong string to this end. Untie your loom from the table leg. You now have the warp bundle neatly threaded through its heddle, knotted at each end, and finished with strings for attachment.

Weaving a Band

Tie one end of the warp to something solid. A door knob often works well. You have a choice for the other end: it could be tied to the back of the chair you will sit on—on the left side if you are right-handed—or to your belt. This is your loom (fig. 5).

The position of the chair with you in it determines the tension on your warp threads: that tension is very important. Shift things about until the warp seems quite tight. Study the photographs here for clues, and if you have troubles with the weaving, first try tightening the warp before trying any other cures.

There will be enough length in this band to weave a sampler of alternatives, before you weave the texture you finally choose. Try at least two weaving threads—one the same in weight as your warp yarn, one thicker. If you do not have a thicker yarn, you can make one by using together several strands of the yarn you used for the warp. Prepare a shuttle with a couple of yards of the first weft you are going to use.

Finding the Sheds

You are now ready to find and open the sheds in your weaving. If there is a single moment that separates folk who weave from all others, it must be this one. Sit down at your warp and push the chair back until the warp is pulled tightly. As you work on your piece, the warp itself will teach you how tight this should be.

5. *A good position for weaving.*

Pull the heddle along the warps so it sits about a foot or so from the knot at your end of things. It won't want to rest in any particular position: arrange it so the slots are vertical. (If it is the kind of a heddle that has one heavier edge, let that be on the bottom.) Lift the heddle up a few inches, shaking it a little as you do so. All the threads in the holes will be forced to rise a little, while the ones in the slots are not required to do so. If one or two do, shake the heddle around a little more and put more tension on the warp. The inner space opened up by this maneuver is the "shed"; it is through here that the weft yarn will pass (fig. 6). Don't weave it in yet, though. Instead, push the heddle down a few inches, so the threads in the holes are forced *below* the slot threads and you see the other shed you can make with this loom (fig. 7). If you wove a yarn through this second shed, it would go over and under the alternate warp threads to those it crossed on the first shed. Thus the necessary interlacements for weaving are automatically made for you, a whole row at a time! Change sheds several times, until you have the knack of it and some idea of how tight the tension on the warp must be for it to open smoothly.

The warps on the loom are pulled together into a knot at each end and are held apart sideways at the place where they go through the heddle. Neither of these widths will determine the width of the finished weaving. That is controlled by the fatness of the warp threads and by the squeeze put on them as you pull the weft yarns into place.

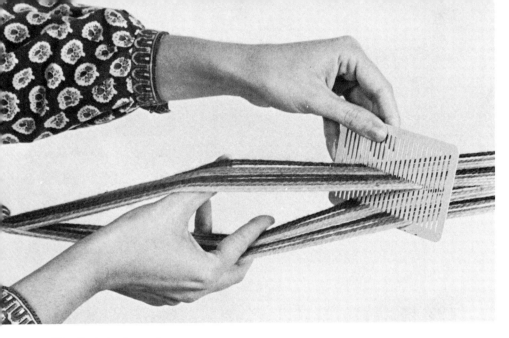

6. *The first shed opening.*

7. *The second shed.*

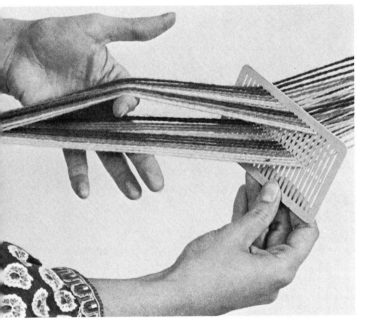

8. *The first weft pass.*

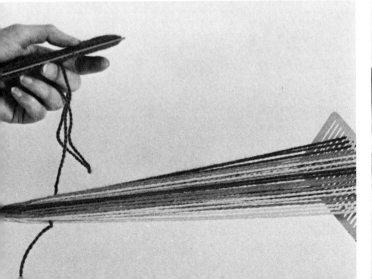

9. Preparing *to weave the next weft.*

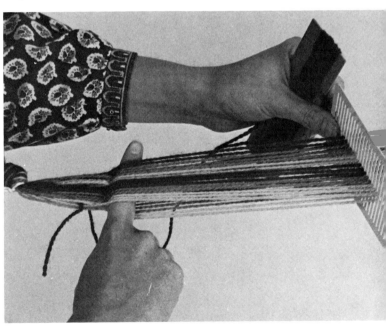

10. *The second weft pass.*

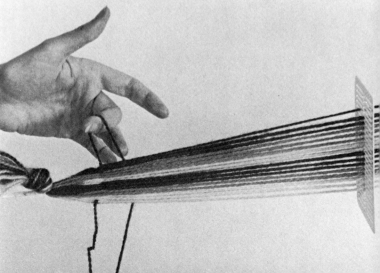

Starting to Weave

Open one of the sheds and stick your finger into the opening between the heddle and the knot at your end of the weaving. Slide that finger toward the knot as far as it will go, opening the shed toward you. Put the end of the weft thread through this opening, letting the free end hang out a few inches, as in Figure 8. The weft should be as close to you along the warp as it will fit.

Change the shed, put your finger into the new shed, and slide it toward you again. It will be stopped by the first weft thread and the crossing of the yarns (fig. 9).

Through this second opening, put the weft thread (fig. 10). The weaving won't look very satisfactory at this point: the warp threads will be bunched together, not spread out as neatly as you would wish. Persevere. Usually it takes a few rows of weaving at the beginning to adjust the band to the width you want, and to be a smooth surface of warp threads with no weft showing. To get your weaving to become smooth and neat, you have to be careful how tightly you pull the weft yarn, watching the place where the weft turns to start the next row as you pull it. You will find that the spreading out of the yarn by the heddle helps you to spread the width of the weaving. You can unravel these first few rows in the final product, so you need not worry about their imperfection.

As you weave along, you'll notice that slipping your finger into the new shed and sliding it back controls how close the weaving threads lie to each other. This process is called "beating in." If you are using a wooden shuttle, you can beat in with that.

Beginning weavers often find that their hardest problem is making the selvedges—the "self-edges," that is, just the edges—of their weaving come out evenly. It is relatively easy to control the selvedges with a warp-faced weave like this one, because you are to pull the weft tightly anyway. There is a tricky way of handling the weft that helps some people get the edges just right: open the shed and weave a yarn through, but don't pull it tight; leave a little loop at the far edge of the weaving, as in fig. 12. Change the sheds and beat in. Now pull the weft thread in the previous shed carefully to the position you wish and weave the new shed, again leaving a loop. (This method will work only for narrow warp-faced structures.)

Weave a few inches, trying to get all these new movements to work for you. Remember that different tensions on the warps make the weaving behave differently. Experiment with tight and loose beating. Prepare to try another yarn as a weft: use a substantially thicker or thinner one. Change color if you think you'll learn something by doing so.

To start a new yarn (fig. 13), break or cut the weaving thread so it is quite short—a broken end is less conspicuous than a cut one—and weave on until the weft won't quite reach across a row. Start the new yarn in that same row, overlapping the yarns. In the photographs we have left the ends long, because we wanted you to be able to see where the yarns were changed. They could be cut off later.

Weave on until you have enough finished to compare this weft to the one you first tried. Try other experiments that come to mind as you weave.

When you have experimented enough, go on to weave your project. If you have decided that you will have fringes on the ends of the band, now weave a piece of cardboard in one shed, wide enough to reserve a space for those fringes (fig. 15). Otherwise, just start weaving the planned part of your project. Feel the rhythm you build up. Feel the texture of the taut warp. Watch the patterns of the changing sheds. Listen to the thread's whisper, the beater's thump. See your weaving grow (fig. 16).

You will notice that you must soon push the heddle away from you to have room to send your weft through the sheds. After a while, you will be weaving so far in front of you that it will begin to be uncomfortable. Then

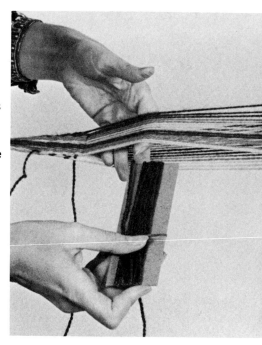

11. *A little way into the weaving.*

12. *The alternate method of pulling the weft tight after the next shed has been opened.*

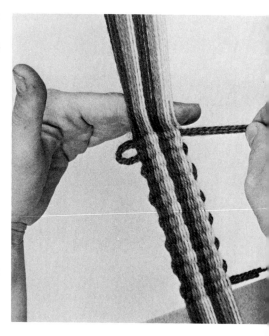

you need to shorten the distance between you and the section of the warp on which you are weaving.

Untie the string that holds your weaving to the chair. Move the chair forward a foot or so and wind most of what you have woven so far around the chair; finish by tying this firmly in place. Adjust the tension and weave on. If you have troubles, look at the last section in Chapter 6; the most common ones are dealt with there. Weave on until you have made a piece as long as you wish. Undo the knots at the warp's ends, pull off your heddle and cut off the experimental part of your weaving. Those sampler bits are well worth keeping to remind you of ideas you tried and as examples of the way specific yarns behave. Finish the ends of the band: there are suggestions of how you might do that at the end of this chapter.

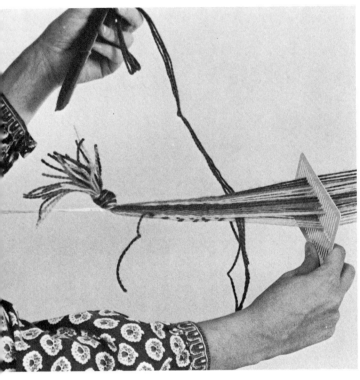

13. *Starting a different yarn.*

14. *Weaving on.*

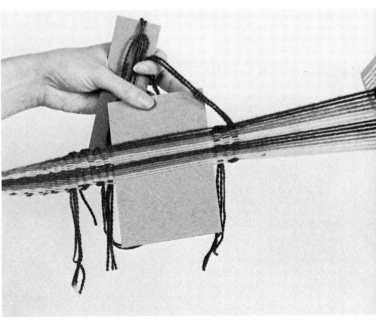

15. *Reserving a few inches of warp to become a fringe.*

16. *Weaving the band.*

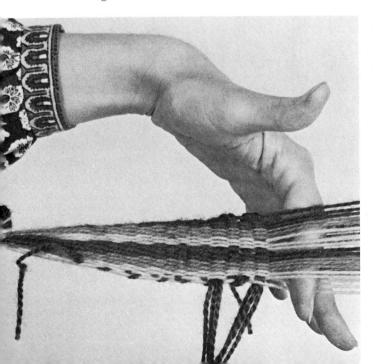

Another Way: A Stick and String Loom

The little rigid heddle loom has been in use in Scandinavia since ancient times. South of the Baltic Sea, another place with a long history of making and using ribbons, a different loom is used for making long narrow strips: the heddle arrangement is a stick and a mesh of string. It is a particularly versatile tool: not only can you make all the parts yourself, but you can also make changes that allow you to weave in different ways.

Neither this loom nor the rigid heddle loom are hard to use once you know how, but the Baltic version is a bit trickier at the beginning. You will find what follows easier to perform if you have first woven or watched the process with the rigid heddle. But if you just can't wait for a rigid heddle to come to hand, then by all means reverse the order and try this way first. You may need to have a little extra patience, but to make up for that think how elegant and convenient it is to use a loom made entirely by you!

This section is organized as though you had woven with the rigid heddle before you came to the stick and string loom. Steps in weaving that are similar in both systems are not repeated here. If you have not yet woven with a rigid heddle, read those instructions with special care, for they contain many details you will need to understand.

2. The first two warp yarns.

Materials You Will Need

A stick: This should be as thick as your thumb or thicker, 6 to 10 inches long, not too rough, not too smooth. A piece of dowel is fine. Something more closely related to a tree is fine, too.

Light string: Use something strong and smooth. Crochet cotton or kite string are good examples.

Two pieces of strong string: Each should be about 4 feet long.

Cardboard: Find a piece about 5 by 7 inches or use a small book.

Weaving yarns: These may be much the same as those suggested for weaving with a rigid heddle.

Shuttles

1. Winding the first warp around the heddle stick.

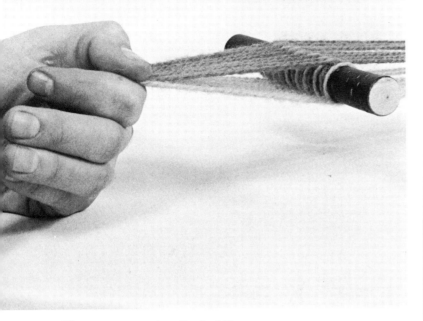

3. The warps wound on the heddle stick.

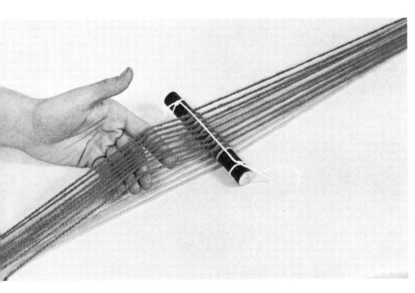

4. A string yoke keeps the warps from sliding off the stick.

5. Picking up the second shed of lighter yarns.

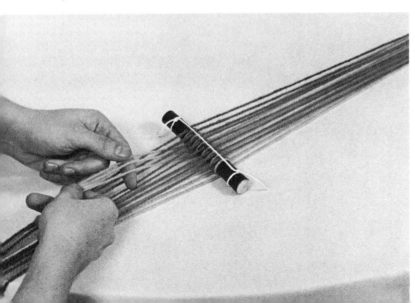

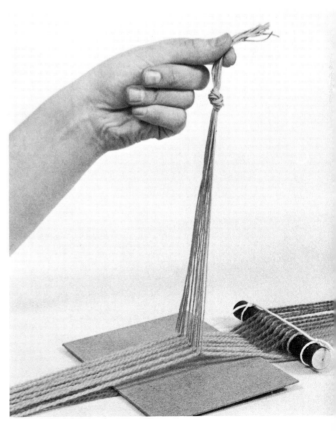

6. The first loop of the string heddles.

7. The finished string heddle.

Preparing the Warp

Cut the warp threads to the length you want, or enough longer to give you a few inches for experiments. Consult the section on warp preparation for the rigid heddle loom. The limitations suggested for a first weaving there—those of length, number of warps, and types of yarn—apply here as well. As you gain experience, you will be able to move beyond those suggestions.

Knot one end of the warps and tie them to a table leg, as before. Separate the first warp thread. Wind this thread around the heddle stick, going first *over* the stick, around and under, and then back over and toward you (fig. 1).

Pick up the second warp and wind it *under* the stick, around and over, and back under toward you (fig. 2). Continue in this way alternating the yarns, having them enter and leave the heddle first over, then under. To help you see what goes on in the figures shown here, we are alternating dark and light threads, the dark always starting and leaving *over* the stick, the light ones *under*. As you proceed, you will see that the stick holds one shed open in the yarns.

When you have wound all the warps on the stick (fig. 3), comb out the warp ends to even the tension and tie the warps together as you did after you had threaded the rigid heddle. Tie the knot to a chair—not necessarily the one you sit on—in order to have the warps lie smoothly on the table during what follows.

In order to keep the warps from sliding off the stick, tie a yoke of string tightly around one end of the stick, pass it over the warps on the stick and then tie it tightly around the far end (fig. 4). This guards against an imaginable accident! Your first shed is held open by this stick.

To find the other shed, you need to pick up the alternate warp yarns by hand, being careful to keep the yarns in their proper order. Think of it as threading your finger through the warps as though you were beginning to weave with no heddles to help (fig. 5).

After you have found the second shed, slip the piece of cardboard (or small book) through the opening to hold it in place, as in Figure 6. Examine the warp for mistakes. The second shed will be opened by pulling on a set of strings. Prepare these string heddles by cutting some light, smooth string into half as many pieces as you have warp threads in your band. Cut them 20 to 24 inches long, all neatly the same length.

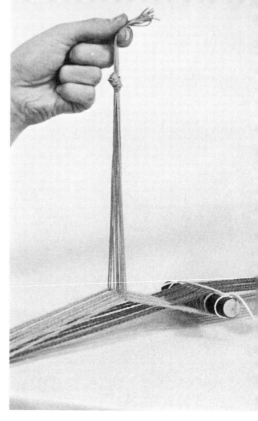

8. The second shed opening.

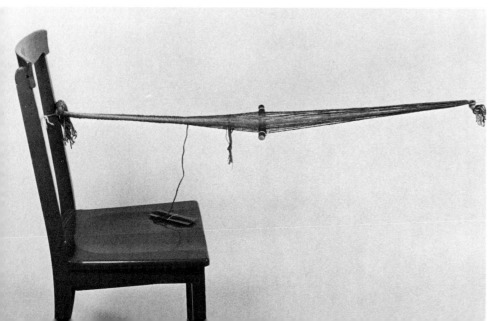

9. The position of the parts of a stick and string loom during weaving. This is a different warp than the one in the previous photos.

Loop one of these string heddles around each warp yarn that goes *over* the cardboard you placed in the second shed. Bring their ends up and align all of these heddle ends. Tie them all together in an overhand knot (fig. 7). When you pull on this knot, half of your warp threads have to come along in the direction of your pull. When you are sure all the correct warps are caught in your string heddle, remove the cardboard (fig. 8).

Weaving the Band

Prepare to weave. Tie the far end of the warp to something that won't budge—the near end to your chair or to yourself as for the rigid heddle. (See fig. 9). Explore some of the characteristics of this new loom. With the warps under some tension, carefully slide first the string heddles and then the stick heddle nearer to you. Notice how the yarns slide around the stick heddle as it moves.

There is another property of this stick heddle you should notice now. You will find that you can spread the warp quite widely apart on the stick and that it will stay that way. This is a real advantage, because the yarns of the warp will not catch on each other as you change sheds: even a fuzzy yarn will open its sheds easily. You will learn how to adjust the width for each kind of yarn as you use it.

When you have the heddles conveniently located, with the string heddle about five inches nearer to you than the stick, arrange the warp so that the knot of the string heddles hangs below the warp, upside down to its position when it was made. Then you can pull down to open that shed.

Explore the sheds. They don't work the same way as the sheds of a rigid heddle. To open the "stick shed," slip your fingers into the shed near the stick and turn them sideways. If there is enough tension on the warp, doing that should raise the yarns that carry the string heddles *through* the alternate yarns. Then you can slip a finger through the opening on the near side of the heddle strings and open the stick shed back toward you, to where you want to be weaving (fig. 10). Your "string shed" opens when you pull down on the string heddles (fig. 11).

Treat the weaving yarn just as you did with the rigid heddle. Review the section "Starting to Weave," which appears earlier in this chapter. It contains the movements you need to proceed with your weaving. When you finish your project you should save both the stick and the string heddles. They have become a valuable loom.

10. *Opening the stick shed past the string shed.*   11. *Opening the string shed.*

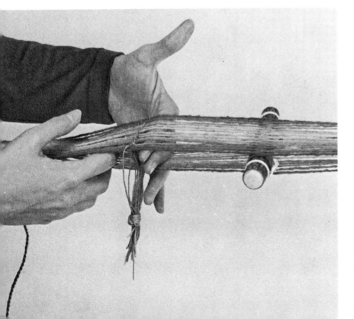

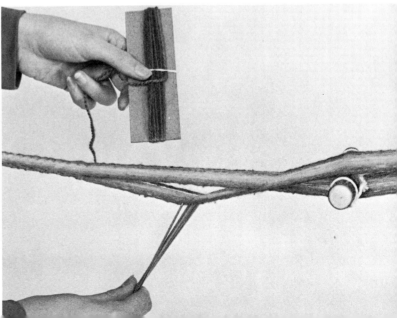

Variations

You can now make weavings of almost any length. In West Africa, narrow warps are prepared in long lengths—say a hundred feet—by setting pegs into the courtyard ground, around which the warps are strung. You may not need to make such extreme lengths of cloth, but you could if you wished.

How wide is practical for this sort of weaving? Look at the distance on your hand from thumb-pit to fingertips. That is the part of your hand you have to enter into the shed of your weaving, so it represents about the width you can easily control. Other weaving techniques, shown in the next chapter, will help you make wider textiles.

You are not limited to warp-faced weaving by the methods shown in this chapter, although you will find that warp-faced weaving happens most gracefully and easily with these looms. If you are careful, you can spread the warp yarns farther apart as you weave, allowing both the warp and weft yarns to show in the finished weaving. You will have to be very careful at the selvedge, where the weft yarn turns and comes back into the next row of weaving. Chapter 6, on plain weave, will give you hints you can apply to these problems. You can even beat the wefts back tightly between your separated warps and produce a weft-faced fabric. The little sampler on p. 40 was woven in these ways.

You do not need to have a chair on which to tie your warp. Some weavers prefer to tie the warp to the front of a belt they are wearing: this is a method considerably older than using chairs. You will find it has disadvantages if you need to answer a ringing telephone, but advantages when you are on a hiking trip.

Braided fringe: If you cannot remember how this is done, Chapter 3 has some drawings to aid you.

Rambu Naha Padjodjang, Maramba Waidjelu, at Melolo, East Sumba weaves narrow bands in a way similar to those shown in this book. Her warp is prepared in a complete circle that can be cut open when the weaving is done. The circular warp goes around a bamboo stick at both the far and near ends: the weaving can be slid around until it's done. A loop of rope goes behind her back and slips over each side of the near bamboo stick. Stick and string heddles similar to those used in this chapter control the sheds. (Photograph by Monni Adams)

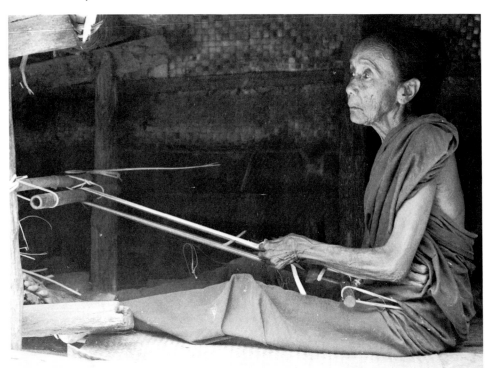

Some Ways To Finish Bands

Assembled: Narrow weavings don't necessarily make narrow cloth. This bag from Central America was made of bands sewn together, side by side.

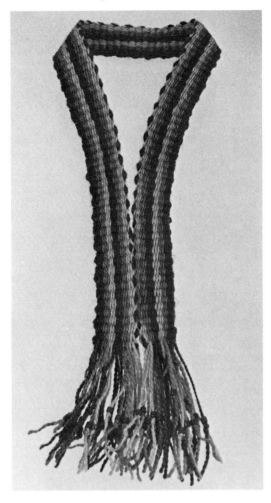

A collar: This was made of the striped band woven at the beginning of this chapter. Glass beads were strung on the plain fringe, each with a knot to hold it on.

Fringed along the Edge: The narrow band was woven in the usual way, but little bundles of yarn were added, woven first into one shed, turned at one of the selvedges, and then woven into the next shed. Repetition of this process produced the fringe.

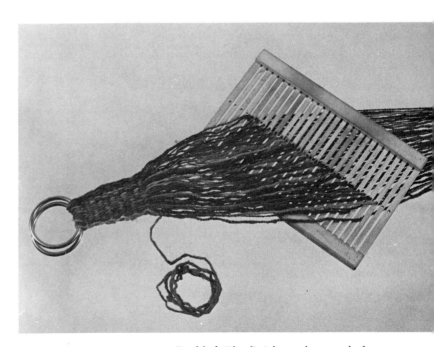

Buckled: The finish can happen before the weaving is made, rather than afterwards! This warp was folded over a belt buckle, in this case made of two plain rings, before the weaving was begun.

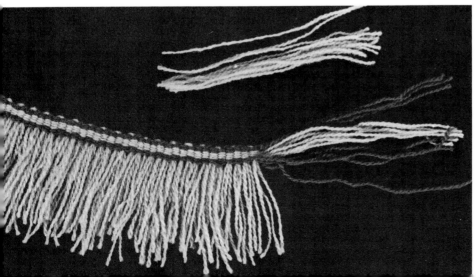

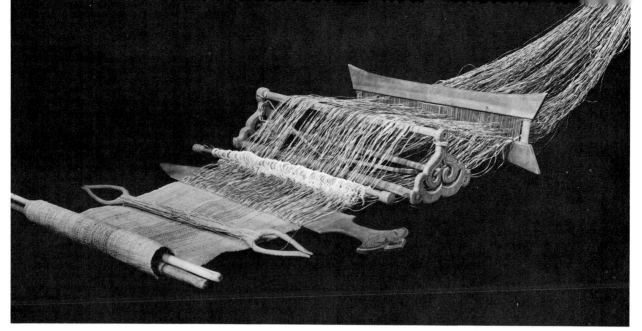

Not all "two-stick" looms are crudely made of unfinished wood. This loom of the Ainu people of northern Japan has each part exquisitely shaped and decorated. The three sticks held together by the triangular scrolled end piece constitute the stick heddle for this loom. The comblike part spreads the warp, which is attached at the far end to a peg; it substitutes for the second loom stick of other looms. The fiber is made of elm-bark, and the cloth is used for clothing. (The Peabody Museum of Archaeology and Ethnology, collected in 1891. Photograph by Hillel Burger)

Many details of her way of weaving show in this picture of a Navaho weaver of rugs. On her vertical loom, the continuous warp is bound to two sticks; the tension can be varied by using the lacing of rope at the top of her loom. She weaves from the bottom up, where the twill cloth she is making can be seen. There is one stick heddle and three string heddles, permitting her to make the sheds she needs for the twill weave. It is possible to see the curve that Navaho weavers prefer in their smooth shed-opening swords. See Chapter 9 for weaving twill yourself. (Photograph by Laura Gilpin)

6. Balanced Plain Weave: Cloth

In any activity, such as weaving, that has a tradition, the more recent methods of working hide those of earlier times. We really do not know how long ago and in how many places weaving was first invented. The knowledge of how to make cloth and baskets is thought to be older than that of how to make ceramics, although our evidence is very sketchy. Cloth and the looms on which it is woven are made of transitory materials, while the fired clay of pots may last for centuries.

In the old world, on the grassy plain to the east of the Taurus mountains in Turkey, lie the ruins of a very old town, now called Çatal Hüyük. Quantities of fine, regularly woven plain-weave cloth, as well as fabric of other weaves, and fabrics with hints of dyeing and colored patterns, were excavated from that place. Those pieces of cloth—some of the oldest known—are 8,000 years old. We can be certain, judging from the amount and kind of weaving found, that some mechanism for keeping order among the threads was used, although we cannot know how complex the loom was.

In the Americas, especially in Peru, very dry conditions have preserved a great richness of perishable materials. There a picture has been pieced together of the transition from rigid baskets to supple cloth through the stages of mats, netted bags, twined fabric, and finally cloth woven on looms with heddles. People were weaving regular cloth in the New World as long ago as in the Old or even longer; we have some scraps of weft-faced stuff dated to 6,000 B.C. that were found in Peru, suggesting that we have been weavers in all lands for a long time.

Looms very like what we know of early looms are still in use today in many parts of the world. We can guess those old looms worked very well since they have changed so little. The basic functional parts of a loom are few. To weave wide cloth—wider than a hand's span—the warp yarns must be held parallel to one another under even tension. Stretching the warp yarns between two sticks has been, and still in many places is, the classic solution to that problem. As weaving machinery grew more complex, the sticks were replaced by heavy bars in a strong framework, wound about with the now longer warp, but their essential function remained unchanged. The controlled tension was provided by the weaver's weight and muscles, by hanging stone weights, or by attaching the two sticks firmly to the ground or other framework. The weight and sturdy construction of renaissance-European and early-American frame looms was required to support the needed tension on the warp. Modern handweavers' framed treadle looms are in that tradition.

Heddle arrangements of various kinds are necessary to provide the weft yarn with easy and efficient access to its path through the warps. The heddles separate the desired warps in their turn, opening alternate sheds wide enough for the passage of the weft-carrying shuttle. Sticks and string—the string already so much a part of the weaver's kit—seem always to have been used to make heddles. Many methods for making heddles, different in detail but similar in concept, are both on old looms and on looms used today by traditional weavers. These loops and twists that pull, sticks that push, yarns that slip past yarns were never obvious to anyone: their existence testifies to the ingenuity and skill of those who invented them. There are many examples of these mechanisms for you to study in

Traditional weavers learn to weave as children from the adults around them. We can learn from those people we know who weave, and also from photographs of weavers. Of the ancient weavers, we can know the woven product, but not all the details about the process of making it. There are a few exceptions, one of which is shown here. The weaver who made the little figures you see teaches us across a large span of years: these figures of a weaver and a child seriously prepare the string heddles on a loom. They were found in the grave of a weaver on the coast of Peru. The box they sit on is a weaver's workbasket, and they are themselves examples of the weaver's art! (The American Museum of Natural History)

the photographs here. Even the metal heddles used in industrial weaving are clearly related to those forms you see here, many of which have persisted unchanged for millennia.

Also necessary to the weaver are the tools that hold the shed open, freeing the hands to manipulate the wefts (themselves organized on a shuttle of some kind), and the tools that compact the freshly laid weft into the texture of the cloth. Here the difference between ancient looms and modern, automatic machinery is the greatest—the old weaver using fingers, sticks and spools; the new technology replacing even the person weaving.

In this chapter are many photographs of weavers at work, using loom types that seem to have changed very little since their invention. You will here learn how to use a loom closely related to theirs. Again, as in the last chapter, two versions of such looms are presented to you: the first a little easier to begin on; the second very versatile in its possible uses. On these you can weave balanced plain weave—the stuff that best fits our inner image of cloth—or weft-faced or warp-faced cloth, enlivened with pattern as you choose. You can adapt this loom, as others have before you, to weave the size of cloth, to accept the kind of yarn, and to use the weaving techniques you have in mind. This loom and what you weave on it connect you with the long past of weavers all over the world. You can master what was possible for them, and even add to their tradition with your own innovations.

When you are five years old in San Antonio, you begin to learn to weave on a loom smaller than that used by an adult, but otherwise the same. The warp is held stretched by a band around the weaver's waist. The geometric brocaded patterns traditional to this town are picked up, a few warp threads at a time, with a pointed stick decorated with a bird form. The young weaver, helped by her older sister, is not expected to weave for long stretches of time. These weaving people, Cakchiquel Indians, live in what seems to be a house of weaving. (San Antonio Aguas Caliente, Guatemala, 1972. Photograph by Aylette Jenness)

In West Africa, women often weave wide cloth, men narrow. This Nigerian woman is weaving a piece that will become half of a wrapper like the one she wears. Her warp is circular, stretched around a beam at top and bottom. She uses string and stick heddles and a wide wooden beater. (Yelwa, Nigeria, 1968. Photograph by Aylette Jenness)

Flora Hernandez helps her daughter Marylena prepare her loom for weaving. A single yarn has been wound around and around to be the warp. Now they even out the tension and organize their heddles. Marylena will weave a brocaded blouse, called a huipil, like those both women are wearing. These huipiles contain patterns both from ancient Mayan and from European sources. (San Antonio Aguas Calientes, Guatemala, 1972. Photograph by Aylette Jenness)

This loom is stretched vertically between pegs in the ground, the tension adjusted with wedges where the two beams cross them. The string heddles and their stick are grand in scale, behind them it is hard to see the details of what the weavers are doing. When the warp lies near the ground like this, the weaver can sit on the part of the weaving that's done. These Nomadic Luristan weavers are probably weaving a rug. (Khorranabad, Iran, 1940s. Photograph by Leon A. Arkus)

A Frame Loom with a Rigid Heddle

Materials You Will Need

A frame: This holds your warp stretched and in good order. A strong, old picture frame is fine. Artists' "canvas stretchers" are excellent and inexpensive, come apart for storage, and can be assembled in various combinations for different sized weavings. A good first set to get might be two 18-inch and two 24-inch ones. While a frame is not absolutely necessary, it is a convenience, for it allows you to stop and start weaving casually and holds the yarns when you are not weaving.

Two sticks: They need to be as wide as your frame or a little wider, to hold your weaving in front of the frame. Sticks collected in the woods are fine as long as they don't break too easily. They should be straight and moderately smooth. Leave the bark on if you can, for its beauty. One-half- or ⅝-inch dowels are fine, too, and are sometimes easier to get.

String and masking tape

A heddle arrangement: The one easiest for new weavers is our old friend, the rigid heddle, from Chapter 5. In this case it will be used in a different manner than it was in making narrow belts: the weaving will be as wide as the heddle. That means that the heddle's width and the spacing of its slots and holes matters. Use a rigid heddle 8 to 15 inches wide, with thread spacing of about 10 to 16 threads per inch. The heddle must fit into the space within the frame. Sources are listed in the Appendix on Tools. If you cannot locate this tool, make and learn to use the stick-and-string heddle described later in this chapter.

Yarn: For your first project, think of using one kind of yarn for both warp and weft, varied perhaps in color to make stripes or plaids, or in textures in some planned or random arrangement. Plied yarn is again a good idea for your first try. Remember that the yarns will have to pass through the holes and slots of your heddle. If the yarns you want to use seem too thin, consider using them double, either plied together or just side by side. The paired yarns needn't be alike either. Yarns are too thick if they won't lie easily side by side at your heddle's spacing.

A shuttle, or several: Cardboard ones are fine.

A beater: This is a flat stick, wide enough to hold the shed open when you send the shuttle through, and longer than your weaving's width. Many people use a ruler as their first beater, and later make one for themselves. On the old looms in museums, the beater is often the most beautiful and the most carefully made part of the loom. See the Appendix on Tools for suggestions on how to make your own beater.

1. Assembling the frame.

Preparing the Warp

Assemble the canvas stretcher frame by pushing the corners together, wedging them firmly, and pushing the frame until all the corners are square (fig. 1). (You do not need the little extra wedge pieces that sometimes come with the frame parts.)

Decide how many warp-strands you will need. An 8 inch width of weaving is satisfactory for a first try with new equipment. An easy way to measure out the length of your warp yarns is to wrap them around your frame (fig. 2). This makes them enough longer than your weaving, producing ends that can be tied. Wind the warp yarn around the frame, counting the length of the frame as one warp. Cut the warps at one end of the frame only, so that each strand when folded in half makes two warps. Lay the bundle of warps near you ready to start warping the loom.

2. Measuring the warp yarns. The frame in this picture is smaller than the 18 by 24 inches we recommend to you. This was done to help make the details in what follows clearly visible in the photographs.

Warping the Loom

Tie the first loom stick across the frame, near one end, as follows: cut two pieces of strong string about 2 feet long and loop them around the end of the frame. The loop shown in Figure 3 works well: it is called a lark's head. Bring the free ends of the string over the stick and around it. As they come back up, divide them, one on each side of the original pair. Tie a shoelace knot over the pair of strings (figs. 4 and 5). Tightening this knot later will let you control the tension of the warp.

Slide the two bowknots toward the sides of the frame, making enough room for the warp between them.

If you feel all butterfingers while you are tying the loom stick on, try taping it in place to the frame sides. The tape will come loose sometime during what follows: discard it when it breaks free.

A good way to arrange yourself for what comes next is to sit at a table, resting the far end of the frame on the table's edge, the near end on your lap. You can manage, too, just by holding the frame on your lap.

Choose the first warp strand, double it and put it over the stick in a lark's head, as in Figure 6. Continue along, spacing the warps roughly as they will be. Change color as you need to for your plan. If you need to change colors at an odd number of warps tie two yarns together at the fold with an overhand knot. Figure 7 shows a set of warps in place.

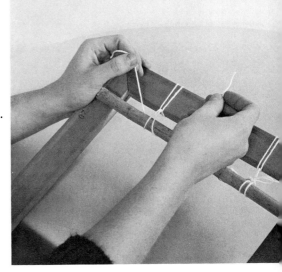

4. *Bringing the string around the loom stick.*

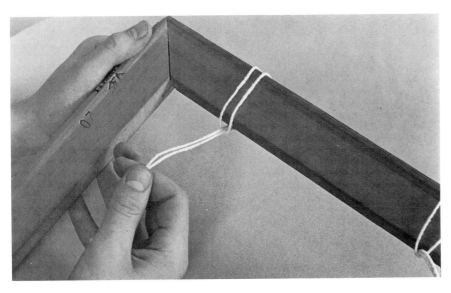

3. *The lark's head loop for the tensioning strings.*

5. *The shoelace knot.*

6. *The first warp pair.*

7. *The warps in place on the first loom stick.*

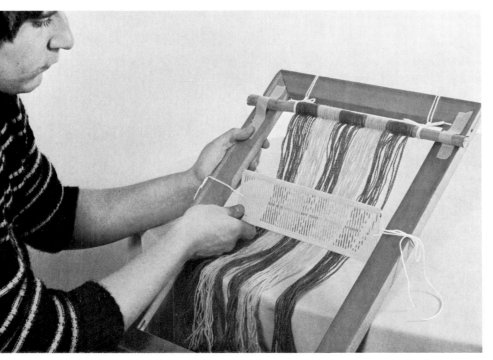

8. *The rigid heddle temporarily tied in place.*

9. *Threading the heddle.*

When the warps are all in place on the stick, temporarily tie or tape the rigid heddle across the middle of the frame (fig. 8). Notice that while the loom stick should rest on top of the frame, the heddle must fit into the space inside it. Starting either at one side or in the middle of the heddle, thread the warps alternately through slots and holes (fig. 9). Work so that the warp threads are centered in the heddle when you finish.

When you are finished, check your threading for mistakes. Grasp the bundle of warps (fig. 10). Lift and lower the heddle, and examine your two sheds. Make any necessary corrections.

Tape and tie the second loom stick the same way as the one at the far end, leaving at this end about 2 inches between the stick and the end of the frame.

Choose a bundle of three or four warp ends from the center of the warp. Comb them through your fingers to pull them out evenly. Bring them toward you over the second warp stick, then around under it. Divide the little bundle in half and bring one half up on each side of itself (fig. 11). Tie a half-hitch—the beginning half of a shoelace knot. Notice that this is the same sort of a knot as the one used to tie the sticks to the loom.

Choose a second bundle to one side of the first: comb and tie it. Continue, as in Figure 12, alternating sides, until all the warps are tied. If you now pat the outspread surface of the warps, you will find they are looser in the middle than at the edges.

Even up the tension, starting at the middle, by loosening the half-hitches, one at a time, pulling the warps tighter and retying them, (fig. 13). Pat the warp to check for evenness. Now take off the temporary tie or tape that holds the heddle to the loom frame.

Try opening the sheds by pulling up and pushing down on the heddle. If the warp seems to wobble up and down loosely when you do that, or if the warps seem to have trouble slipping past each other as you change sheds, tighten the whole warp. To do that, loosen the two bows that hold on the far loom stick, one at a time, and retie them, pulling the dowel closer to the frame.

The warps should not be left this tight except when you are weaving. Loosen them by reversing the same procedure whenever you stop weaving for more than an hour or two. You can collapse your loom for transport, as nomadic people do, even in the middle of a weaving, by removing the four strings that hold the loom sticks to the frame, disassembling the frame, and rolling up the warp on its two sticks.

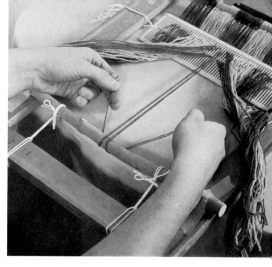

11. *Beginning to tie the warps to the second loom stick.*

12. *Tying the near end of the warp yarns.*

13. *Retying the warp yarns to even the tension.*

10. *Checking the threading.*

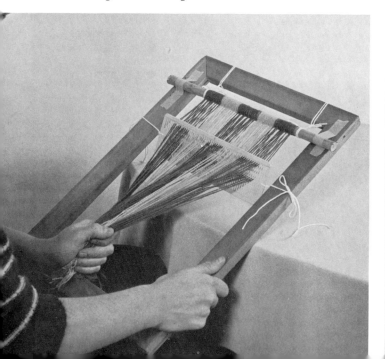

Preparing the Weft

Prepare the weft, winding the yarns you will use on shuttles. For this first project, it is a good idea if the yarns are the same as the ones you used for the warp. If you use cardboard shuttles, make them as long as the weaving is wide or a little less by about 1½ inches.

Starting to Weave

You are almost finished! For most weaving of small projects, you will find it takes more time to prepare the warp than to make the final interlacing of the threads.

To weave, try sitting at a table with the loom resting between your lap and the table's edge. Have your wound shuttles, and your beater—is it a ruler?—at hand.

Open a shed by raising or lowering the heddle, and slip the beater between the warps (fig. 14). After the beater is in, turn it edgewise to open the shed even further. It should stay in place when you let go of the heddle, freeing your hands for what follows. Send the shuttle through this shed, letting some inches of weft dangle free at the beginning (fig. 15).

Remove the beater and open the second shed. Slide the beater in, and use it held flat to push the first weft yarn as near to the knots tied on the shed stick as it will go (fig. 16). The warps may not space out evenly for the first few wefts; you could ravel out the uneven weaving when the piece is finished. Having "beaten" the first yarn in place, turn the beater edgewise, to open the new shed. Return the shuttle back through the weaving. Pay attention to how the yarn is pulled at the edge of the weaving: the smoothness at the edge of your cloth will be largely determined by how the weft yarn turns. It should lie snug but not too tight.

Holding the shuttle end of the weft, arrange the weaving yarn so that it crosses the loom on a diagonal, as you see in Figure 17. That slanted path the weft takes across the loom is slightly longer than a path straight across would be. When the yarn is beaten straight, that extra length is distributed as the ups and downs of the weft's path across the warp. This extra ease is another of the things that keeps the edges of your weaving from pulling in.

Change sheds. Slide the beater into this shed and use it to beat the diagonal yarn into place next to the first yarn, before you set it on edge to proceed (fig. 18). You now can understand why this tool is called the beater. Try to make the spacing of the weft yarns match that of the warps.

The warps may still be bunched up, but after a few more rows, the weaving should appear even. If this is not happening, retie the strings that hold the loom sticks to the frame so that the warps are held under greater tension. Another problem that often appears at the time you begin weaving is a shed that resists opening because the warp threads seem to stick to each other. More tension on the warps is the first thing to try for curing that as well. Refer to the section called "Troubles" at the end of this chapter when you need help.

If the edges are pulling in a little bit, that is all right. If you look at woven pieces in museums, you will see this has happened to weavers more experienced than you. If your edges are pulling in too much, check the Weaving Narrows section in "Troubles." Remember that you can ravel out your weaving, as did Penelope when she was awaiting Ulysses' return, and make a fresh start.

14. *Slipping the beater in the first shed.*

15. *With the beater on edge, the shuttle has passed through the shed.*

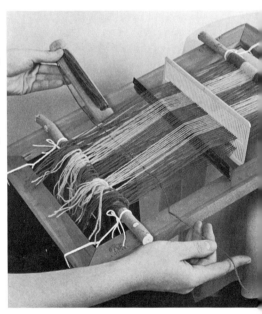

16. *Beating the first weft into place.*

Weaving Along

After each weft pass, beat the weft yarn in. For balanced plain weave, the weft threads should be about as close to each other as the warp threads are. You need to judge this by eye as you go along.

Continue the rhythm of weaving: open shed, beat in, beater on edge, weft pass. If you run out of yarn on the shuttle, overlap the new yarn a few warps' width, as you did with the weft-faced bags in Chapter 4.

To change to a yarn of a different color, break off the old yarn an inch or two past the edge of the weaving, send it around the edge warp and back into the same shed (fig. 19). Change sheds, then weave the first pass of the new yarn, leaving the free end dangling from the opposite edge. Pick it up and weave it back into its shed, going around the outermost warp. Or you can just overlap the yarns for a change of color somewhere along the row of weaving. It is surprising how these small irregularities are lost in the texture of the repetitive weaving.

Mistakes, happily, are often noticed just before they are actually consummated. For instance, you might see a single warp lying in the wrong shed while you are beating, before the shuttle goes through. You can fix that. If you first see a mistake a few rows after it has happened you have a harder decision: to return or not? Not every irregularity is wrong in the final result; use your personal judgment.

In plain weave the warp thread travels in a sinuous path over and under the weft yarns, causing the warp tension to become tighter and tighter as you weave. You will need to loosen the warp tension for better weaving at some point. And remember to loosen the tension whenever you stop for a few hours or more.

18. Beating back a diagonal weft.

19. Ending a yarn.

17. The weft yarn in the diagonal position.

73

20. *The shed space becomes narrow.*

21. *Cutting the cloth off the loom.*

Ending Up and Going On

As you come close to the far end, you will have trouble getting your shuttle and beater to fit into the small space left (fig. 20). If you are determined to weave as far as possible, you can switch to a narrower shuttle and beat back your weaving with a comb. In many parts of the world, weavers do not bother with these last few rows of weft, while in other places they weave to the very end, finally sewing the last wefts into place. No matter which way you work, you will eventually come to a place where you decide you have finished.

You can remove your weaving from the loom in two ways: either cut the warps, as in Figure 21, near the sticks or take the sticks off the frame and slide the warp loops off the sticks. Either way your cloth can have fringe.

Cloth just off the loom has an oddly stiff feeling; the fibers are still influenced by the tension they have known. To transform your woven piece into real cloth, wash it: gently, preferably with a drop of detergent in the water. Let it dry; iron it carefully if you think that will improve it. After it is washed, the edges will have little tendency to ravel.

Study your piece when you have finished it. Feel its texture. Hold it up to the light, looking through it. Fold it, stretch it, smell it! The better you come to know it, the more it can teach you what to try next.

Your first piece on this loom may have the general air of an experiment. You had so many novel techniques to master, and you were using yarns in a way so new to you that the final result probably just happened. Have a plan in mind for your second try: you know much more now.

22. *The cloth.*

A Frame Loom with Stick and String Heddles

A time will come when you do not want the limitations determined by the rigid heddle: the fixed warp spacing, its maximum width, or its restriction of two sheds only. You can master another way to make sheds work, using heddles made of sticks and strings and be free to weave however you choose. Stick and string heddles belong to the traditional world of weavers. In every part of the world where weaving was done, mechanisms similar to these were used by all who made cloth. The pictures at the beginning of this chapter show you that this tradition is still alive today. And you can carry on that tradition as you join in using it.

Although you can weave with stick-and-string heddles before using a rigid heddle, you will have to master more new details all at once. If you do proceed in that order, read the previous section through carefully, visualizing each step, trying in your imagination to weave the small piece of checkered cloth shown there. What is common to the two methods is not repeated here.

Materials You Will Need

Two heddle sticks: These can be just like your loom sticks, or of a
    somewhat lighter weight. They should be longer than the width of the
    weaving.
String heddle loops: Make these of strong, smooth, light string: crochet
    cotton, kite string, or fishing line are candidates. You can use these
    loops over and over if you make them in a standard manner. For your
    first project, you will need half as many string heddles as you have warp
    threads. Cut these heddle strings about 15 inches long. You need to tie
    loops of a standard size, about 9 to 12 inches around. Find a rigid book,
    a box or a block of the right size. One by one, tie the heddle strings
    around this jig, using a square knot pulled up evenly and tightly (fig. 1).
    After the knot is tied, trim off the extra string, leaving about ½ inch. If
    you try to tie the knot with only this much to spare, you can't tighten it
    securely enough to hold.
(The other materials and tools are the same as those needed to weave with
    a rigid heddle):

A frame	Yarn
Two loom sticks	Shuttles
String	A beater

Setting Up the Loom

Prepare the warp yarns as before—this time skipping the rigid heddle—stretching the warp between the two loom sticks before the sheds are organized (fig. 2). The distance between the warp threads will be governed by how they are arranged on the loom sticks. Make the spacing you think you will want, remembering that you can adjust this again later. You can hold this spacing by laying a piece of masking tape across the warp on the loom sticks. You may feel you don't need that.

One of the most subtle and difficult matters for new weavers to judge is that spacing. For balanced plain weave, the distance between warps can be guessed at by winding the warp threads around a piece of cardboard in such a way that you can just see the cardboard between the windings. Count the threads in an inch's width and try that gauge. Try a more open spacing than you might otherwise for your first try. With string heddles, it is easy to make adjustments in the warp width, after you have woven the first few rows, by sliding the warp yarns along the loom sticks.

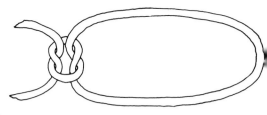

A heddle string with a square knot.

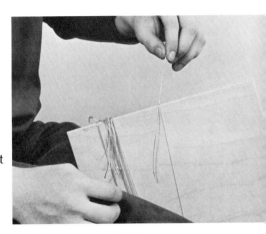

1. Tying string heddle loops.

2. The stretched warp. This frame is 18 by 24 inches, it has been warped with a random arrangement of yarns of many textures, a set of yarns better for a second weaving project than for a first.

3. Using the heddle stick to find the first shed.

4. *Using the beater to find the second shed.*

5. *The first string heddle passing under the first warp of this set.*

Prepare the first shed by working one of the heddle sticks over and under alternate warps across the loom (fig. 3). Tie a string yoke from end to end of this stick to keep it from sliding out of its shed. When the warp is under tension, this stick heddle holds open a shed into which you can slide the beater. This is the stick shed.

The second shed—the string shed—will be made between you and the heddle stick you have just inserted. While that first shed is always held open by its stick, the new shed must be able to appear and disappear.

To find it, weave the beater across the loom, over the warps that are above in the first shed, under those below (fig. 4). When you have worked your way across, check carefully that all yarns are in their correct order. Let the beater lie there identifying the threads that lift to make this shed during what follows.

As in Figure 5, slip one of the prepared heddle strings under the leftmost warp that lies on top of the beater. The circle of heddle string will make a loop on each side of that warp. Pick up *both* of those loops and slip them on your second heddle stick (fig. 6). If you now lift the stick that first warp thread is also lifted. Repeat this across the row, a string heddle for each warp that lies over the beater (fig. 7). When the row is done, tie a string around one end of the stick, send it over the heddle loops to the far end, and tie it there as a yoke to secure the string heddles (fig. 8).

Check to see that when the string heddle stick is lifted, the alternate warps lift to open the second shed; then remove the beater.

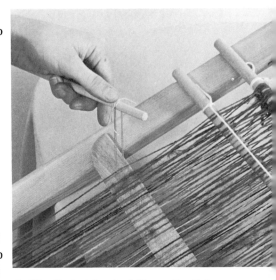

6. *The first string heddle on its stick.*

7. *The string heddles.*

Playing with the Sheds

These sheds won't work unless the warp is under considerable tension, so increase the tension. To open the first shed, bring the stick heddle close to the string heddles. Strum across the warps with the back of your finger once or twice and the shed should open (fig. 9). Slip the beater in and turn it on edge to make room for the shuttle (fig. 10).

To find the second shed, push the stick heddle away from you and lift the string heddle stick (fig. 11). The alternate shed should rise, perhaps with a little strumming to encourage it.

When your loom is light and your warp is tight, there is a tendency for your whole loom to rise as you lift your string heddle stick. If you have that problem, one way to hold it in check is to place your loom in the angle between a table top and the narrow board that runs under it.

New sheds are usually "sticky" when you first start weaving—the fine fuzz on the warp yarns tangles together. This usually improves after the first few inches of weaving. If it doesn't, consult the section on "Troubles" at the end of this chapter.

Weaving

Manipulating the weft yarn on a loom with stick-and-string heddles is much like weaving on a rigid heddle loom, so continue on in ways you already know. This is carefully described in the first half of this chapter. Refer back if you need to.

Our emphasis so far has been on the structure of woven cloth and on the machinery that enables cloth to come into being. The tools that did the work have been very simple, very direct: sticks and string mostly. This simplicity of means tells you that you are working close to the source, in a way that is common to all weaving, from the simple devices of antiquity to the most elaborate machinery of today. What you now understand about weaving applies to all weaving ever made.

Working with these looms is good preparation for using any other kind of loom, even for thinking through loom variations that you make for yourself. Don't go beyond these simple two-stick looms never to return: these are so quickly responsive, so versatile, so under your control, that you would have lost a valuable tool.

8. *Tying the yoke in place.*

9. *Strumming the warps to open the stick shed.*

10. *Inserting the beater.*

11. *The string heddle shed.*

12. *Weaving on.*

Variations

Looms that use heddles of sticks and strings are enormously versatile. You can weave variations of warp- and weft-faced fabric, as well as weaves that are in between in their characteristics. Navaho rug weavers, using looms similar to ours, arrange their warps farther apart: weft-faced weaving appears. Closer warps will produce the opposite effect. You will have to experiment with these spacings and with the results produced by dissimilar weights of yarn for warp and weft to become familiar with the possibilities.

The third part of this book, "Pattern," will show you many variations that can be woven on a stick and string loom. A useful property of these looms is their possibility for more than two sheds. Chapter 9 will show you how this is done.

You can weave larger cloths than you have been shown so far. Dowels and canvas stretchers are very inexpensive; by having several sets it becomes possible to weave in a variety of sizes. Subtract 5 inches from the width of a canvas stretcher frame to know the maximum width you can weave on that frame. But the length of the frame does not determine the length of cloth you can weave on a given frame. The warps are, after all, attached to the loom sticks, not to the frame. If you make a warp almost twice the length of a given frame and then wrap that warp around the frame, warp tension can by applied by tying the two loom sticks to each other, using the same adjustable knot as before. Any part of the warp can be turned to any position on the frame by loosening the tension and moving the warp around, so it is always easy to have the growing edge of the weaving in a convenient relationship to the weaver. An 18-by-24-inch frame then easily produces cloth 13 by 40 inches, and you can think of weaving scarves and clothing even with this first loom. Other pairings of different size canvas stretcher frames will have other maximum possibilities.

In the photos shown on the next page, and in many at the beginning of this chapter, weavers work on warps attached to two loom sticks, but those sticks are not attached to a four-sided frame. In one alternate arrangement, the back-strap loom, the warps are attached at one end to a fixed point and at the other end to the weaver's own body. Loom and weaver become one; the muscular tension of the weaver enters the textile.

If you examine these photographs, you will see many hints that will aid you to weave in this manner. Notice especially the postures of the weavers: they can all actively change the warp's tension by the body's motion.

Longer weavings. Left: The back side of a weaving longer than its frame. The two warp sticks have been tied to each other instead of to the canvas stretchers. They are tied with the knots used before that permit easy adjustments of warp tension. The weaving is partially finished here. Right: A side view with the loom in position for weaving. The entire warp can be moved around the frame.

Ana Hida of Pajete, a weaver in East Sumba, Indonesia, weaves in plain weave a warp that has been elaborately prepared by tie-dyeing. She weaves a plain dark weft yarn through the warp; it softens the colors but does not blur the pattern. You can see detailed comparisons between her processes and yours. Here the stick heddle is in the near position, and the beater holds the stick shed open. (Photographs by Monni Adams)

The string shed is lifted. The weaver leans forward, releasing tension on her warp.

Troubles

Weaving Narrows

It is often difficult to keep your weaving from pulling in at the edges and becoming narrower as you weave along. The Navaho woman who was weaving the saddle blanket shown here had this problem, too. Her weaving stabilized at a narrower width, and she wove on. There is usually a "natural" width for a specific yarn and technique.

To overcome this problem, be careful not to pull the weft yarn too tightly as you come around the selvedge. Lay the weft diagonally across the warp before you beat it into place. A steeper diagonal distributes more yarn across the width. Enough tension along the warp's length also prevents the yarns from pulling in.

If these methods fail, pin your weaving to a "stretcher" rod just back from the growing edge of the weaving. That requires a stick—one that will accept thumbtacks—as wide or wider than the width you aim for, and a couple of pins or thumbtacks. Pin the stick behind the weaving, with the two pins near the selvedge and the weaving stretched to that desired width. After you have woven a few rows, "walk" the stick nearer to the active row by shifting one pin at a time. You may need to keep this up for the entire weaving or you may be able to dispense with it once you have "set your width."

Holding the weft yarn in place as it turns at the selvedge.

A Navaho saddle blanket, unfinished, still on its loom. Notice the interesting three-color weft-faced twill weave, the four heddles (one stick, three string), the continuous warp held to the warp sticks by a string, and the narrowing at the start of the weaving. For using more than two heddles, see Chapter 11. (The Peabody Museum of Archaeology and Ethnology. Photograph by Hillel Burger)

Controlling the width of a woven piece. The Mexican woman who was weaving this cloth used a hollow reed, cut to just the right width, as her stretcher. Two thorns slipped into the reed's open ends take the place of your thumbtacks. She has attached this mechanism to the back of her weaving, which we see here. (In the photographic series of the East Sumba weaver, you can also see such a stretcher, this time carried along on the front of the weaving. it is the slender stick across the weaving nearest to the weaver.)

Broken Warp Thread

If a warp thread breaks, you need to replace it before you can continue weaving. For this you will need a needle, preferably one with a blunt point—a "crewel" needle—and a new warp yarn, long enough to stretch from the active edge of the weaving to the far warp stick, plus a few inches for attachment. Figures 1, 2, and 3 shown here illustrate the steps in replacing a broken warp thread.

Knot the new warp yarn to the old, broken one at the far end of the loom, where the warp goes around the warp stick. This places the knot outside of the area to be woven. Thread the new warp along the path belonging to the broken yarn, over or through the correct heddle opening, keeping it between the correct pair of warp yarns all along its path.

When you come to the edge of the weaving, where wefts cross the warps, thread the warp onto the needle and weave the needle toward you into the cloth. Follow the broken warp, darning over and under the same weft yarns as it does. After about an inch of darning, pull the new warp yarn through. The old and new warp yarns overlap here. The overlap will not be noticeable in the finished work. The unwoven part of the broken warp thread—between the break and the edge of the weaving—can be allowed to hang free until you have woven farther. Later it can be cut off.

Adjust the tension of the new warp yarn by pulling on the needle end. To hold that tension even as you weave, use the needle as a cleat: unthread it and tuck it into the cloth near the new warp's end; make the new warp temporarily secure by winding it around the needle's ends in a figure-eight.

Ignoring the loose broken end, weave on for a couple of inches, until all is secure. Remove the needle and cut off the loose ends. If many warps break, you may have started with very uneven warp tension, or you may be using too weak a thread for a warp. Yarns will soon teach you their suitability for use as warps.

"Sticky" Shed, Will Not Open Easily

Unlike the problem with a weaving's width, this one leaves no evidence for us to see in textiles displayed in museums. You can be sure though that it has been a problem for weavers of all times. Especially when you begin working on a new weaving, the fuzzy down on your warp threads becomes entangled, and the sheds will not open gracefully.

There are several ways to go about correcting the problem.

Pat the warp. Is the tension even? If the warps bunch up in sections, the tension is uneven and requires adjustment.

Is there enough tension overall? It seems odd, but extra tension in one direction seems to help the shed to open in the other direction.

If you are weaving with a stick and string band loom, try spreading the warp out wider on the stick heddle. The extra distance between the individual warps should help.

Try dampening your warps with water or even with starch to slick down their fuzz while you are working on the cloth. Wash out any starch when you have finished weaving.

Some yarns have just too much fur, lumps, loops, or other trim to work well as warps. Try to design in such a way that those yarns can be wefts instead. This diagnosis can't always be made just by looking, though. Some yarns that look impossible turn out to have just the right slipperiness to work well. Hard-won experience is the way to understanding.

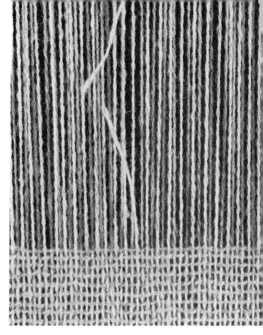

1. A broken warp thread.

2. "Darning" in the new warp.

3. Using the needle as a cleat to secure the new warp yarn temporarily.

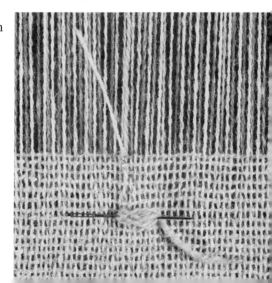

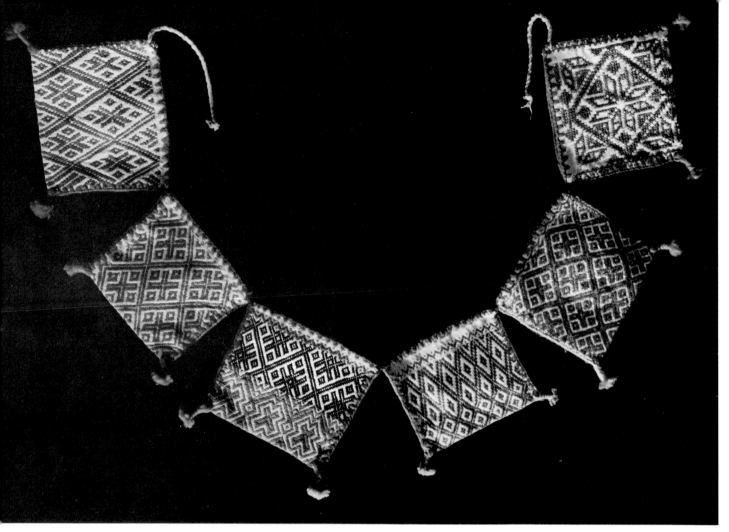

This traditional string of bags from Mexico gave its maker the opportunity to explore variations of similar patterns. (The Peabody Museum of Archaeology and Ethnology. Photograph by Hillel Burger)

The striped end of a white wool sash from Kashmir. The body of the sash is twill-woven. (Peabody Museum of Archaeology and Ethnology. Photograph by Hillel Burger)

Pattern

Having come to understand looms, the tools that aid in transforming yarn to textile, you can now begin to explore pattern, the decoration woven into cloth. Combining yarns of different colors make patterns; so does combining yarns with different weights or substances or textures. There are other kinds of patterns made by changing the interlacement of the yarns. In either case, some patterns are exact, following precise rules; others are freer, allowing variation within limits.

As you explore patterns, you will notice again and again that choosing one set of actions turns out to have consequences broader than you expect. A change of one kind can require—or prevent—some other change as the orderly structure of the cloth grows. These interrelationships are a part of the woven web, but they are at bottom mathematical; they grow naturally out of the modular and ordered array of the woven elements. (As one example, think of the way the yarns in plain weave are a model for the odd and even numbers.) The weaving of patterns brings you into close contact with those mathematical relationships, for all that it does not require you to deal with many numbers. You can, if you wish, take special notice of this, and enjoy what happens.

Anyone who weaves understands these relationships to some degree, or the cloth would not get made. It may feel easy to have the weaving "come out that way," yet it is not simple. All weavers, while manufacturing a material web, are exploring a subtle intangible web at one and the same time. This was as true for the first weavers as it is for you. Those weavers who first invented the new patterns instead of learning them from another weaver were surely also exploring the earliest mathematical structures beyond simple counting. For human weavers, weaving has always been more than spiders' games.

Only a few of the many possible kinds of pattern are to be found in this book. Those few were chosen to be as different at possible, while at the same time being rewarding to explore. Although all of these ways of making patterns have already been used by weavers in many places, they so invite variation that you, too, can change them to meet your own needs.

The patterns are presented less as a set of rules to follow than as a set of relationships to understand. The aim is to have you see how the basic structures are formed, so that you can invent patterns for yourself, as weavers have always done. Understanding of this sort will allow you to learn from other sources as well. After you have explored some of what is presented here, you should begin to be able to analyze any textile that delights you, to understand the logic of its structure, and to take your own use from it. You will need no new equipment: the tools you have used already in this book are adequate for the new tasks. And if you should use other looms than those presented here, you would still be able to weave the pattern techniques this book suggests.

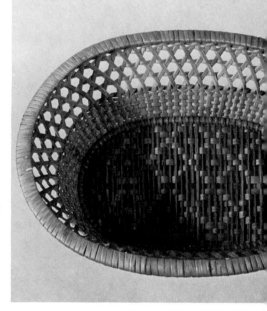

Baskets often display interesting weaves, some of which can be explored with loom-woven cloth. The bottom of the oval basket (top) is interlaced in a twill arranged to show diamonds. The pattern of the other basket (bottom) is not, strictly speaking, a twill.

There is little chance that you will want to use every kind of pattern shown here, or that you will want to use them in their traditional ways. Choose those that lead in directions which interest you. This book uses the traditional patterns as examples, not only because they are a natural starting point for the understanding of pattern, but also because keeping our examples close to tradition preserves your freedom to move beyond it in your own way. As you explore these forms, feel how much freedom of choice is available to you; how you come to be in control of where, how much, in what juxtaposition your own use of pattern happens. Use pattern as you use yarns—by choosing for yourself.

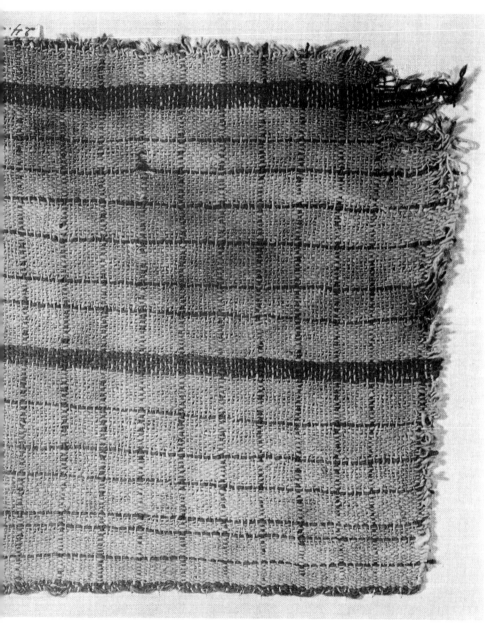

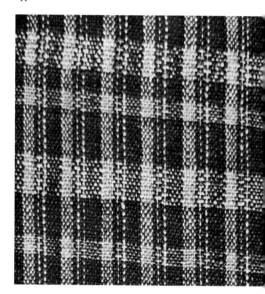

Many colors and weights of yarns in a random relationship produce a plaidlike effect.

Blue and cream-colored cotton threads repeat with one pattern for the warp, another for the weft. The result is a plaid cloth. Japanese, 20th cent. (The Museum of Ethnography, Basel)

The indigo-blue warp is interspersed with six groups of white threads in this cloth, while the weft is entirely blue yarn. The result is a striped cloth. Nigeria, 1960s.

A single dark thread, appearing with some regularity in both the warp and the weft, makes a series of lines across the cloth. At one place half a dozen dark threads, side by side, build a wider dark band. Pre-Columbian Peru. (The Museum of Fine Arts, Boston)

84

7. Stripes, Checks, and Plaids

The structure of a cloth of plain weave is just what its name implies: plain. The warp as well as the weft threads repeat the same over-one, under-one path regularly throughout the cloth. Even so, the cloth need not appear monotonous: its appearance can be altered without changing its plain-weave structure by varying the color or the texture of individual threads. A great number of effects are possible: weavers have been exploring them for a long time, always finding new combinations of color, scale, and rhythm.

A single yarn of a contrasting color produces a dotted line across the cloth; repeat the line farther on and stripes appear; lay several of the contrasting yarns next to each other and the thin stripe broadens. Send such contrasting yarns in the other direction, be it warp or weft, and checks and plaids spring out. Vary the yarns randomly for one effect; arrange them according to strict rhythms for many more. Use two colors or sizes or textures; or use many. The photos on the facing page show four cloths of plain weave whose patterns are made by varying the color and texture of the woven yarns.

You need to know no special tricks to weave such patterns. Experiment with various juxtapositions of color, of weights of yarn, and of fibers that please you. Think about the rhythmic qualities of different repeats, and about their scale in relationship to the size of your yarns and the finished fabric. Remember too that the fabric will exist off the loom: different yarns can change the feel of the final cloth. Look in the world about you, not only at fabrics but also at books on a shelf, city maps, or fields of grasses for ideas of how to design these patterns.

Stripes and their intersections may be easy to organize and simple to weave, but they are not trivial. The effects you make can be subtle or bold, bright or rich or quiet. They can appear as characteristic of your work alone or can carry echoes of other cultures, which have all produced their own versions of this way to embellish cloth.

Keep a notebook or a box of your weaving projects, yarns, samplers, ideas for future weaving, resource lists, and clippings of forms or colors that catch your eye. Sometimes you can insert an actual sample of weaving, for instance, the preliminary length you wove when making a band, but often you have no part of a weaving to spare. It then becomes useful to have a drawing of the construction of a weaving, showing whatever is needed to recreate the salient parts of the textile.

The crossing of even warp and weft stripes produces checkered squares. Here is the pillow you saw being woven in chapter 6. There are light stripes and dark ones, yet this does not result in only light or dark squares in the weaving; there are areas of mixed light and dark as well. Where these three "tones" appear depends on the geometrical arrangement of warp and weft. The areas of intermediate tone, where the warp is one color and the weft another appear especially lively, showing different shades when viewed at different angles. Checkered gingham or traditional red-and-white tablecloths show this effect as well.

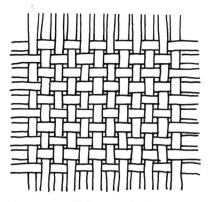

Weavers call these little sketches "pattern drafts." "Draft," after all, means a drawing. We shall use a very simple convention here, one that lets you see the individual yarns clearly. The warp threads are always shown in the up-and-down position on the page, the same position in which you see them when you are weaving.

Using Thin Air

In weaving, the spacing of yarns—the distance between them—is always important. Changes in spacing affect the physical properties of the cloth as well as its visual form. Keep experimenting with this as you weave, especially with the yarns you use most. Sometimes even small changes will make interesting differences.

The changes that occur as you vary the spacing are often unpredictable: many marvels are hidden just beyond easy guessing. The photograph below shows two cloths that look very distinct from each other. Yet they are most closely related: the structure, the materials, the number of warp threads are the same in both; only the spacing between the warp threads is different, causing one version to be wider than the other. That spacing varies from moderately open in one example to moderately close in the other: this difference changes the entire character of the cloth.

You need not even change the color of your yarn or its weight to get rewarding effects in this manner. Try widening the spacing between the yarns even farther, to create open air between the threads. You are adding that most gossamer filament of all—empty space. But be careful. Weaving made entirely of that stuff is fit only for emperors' clothes!

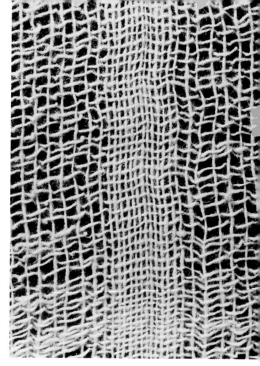

A detail of a wool scarf from Ireland with variable open warp spacing

A texture produced by white yarns of different weights.

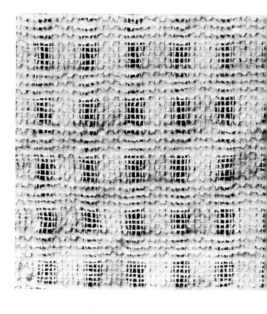

Here are two textiles using the same warp: the top one was woven with a close warp spacing, the bottom one with a looser spacing. The resulting differences in the look of the fabric seem surprising. In the cloth at the top of the photograph, the structure has become predominantly warp-faced. (This fabric also shows the interesting change made in the appearance of plain weave cloth by interspersing a thicker thread among the thinner ones.)

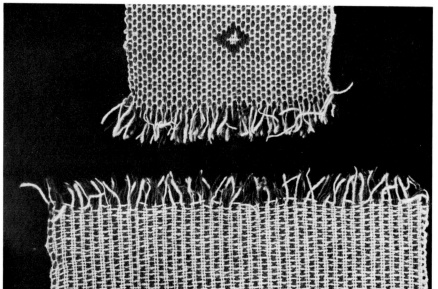

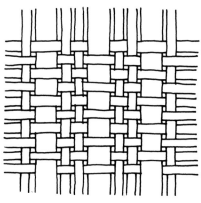

A draft of the cloth in the photo to the left. The warp threads are vertical, and the cloth is plain weave.

Variations

Variations in yarn weight and denseness of spacing may produce surprising effects, but the simple change of yarn color alone can produce unexpected results as well. While a single contrasting yarn makes a dotted line, placing several such rows of weaving near each other produces a result that is much less linear. If you alternate those colored rows with ones of the background yarn, the striped effect disappears entirely, to be replaced by an interesting all-over color texture.

This effect, and others like it, can be woven with fine yarns or heavy ones; the result will look very different as you explore the variations. You will find that different thicknesses of yarn change the resulting cloth drastically. The effect may appear boldly before your eyes or occur just below your ability to discriminate the individual threads. The effects can be similar to those created by Pointillist painters of the nineteenth century, who painted without blending their colors on the palette, but put dot by dot of vibrant color side by side on the canvas. Each dot was small enough so that when you stepped back a few paces, you saw not dots, but yourself blended the color as the artist intended. Weavers can play such games, too.

The draft here shows a single contrasting yarn, its horizontal position indicating it is a weft yarn. The draft is a convention used by weavers to record a pattern. You will see similar drafts in other weaving books.

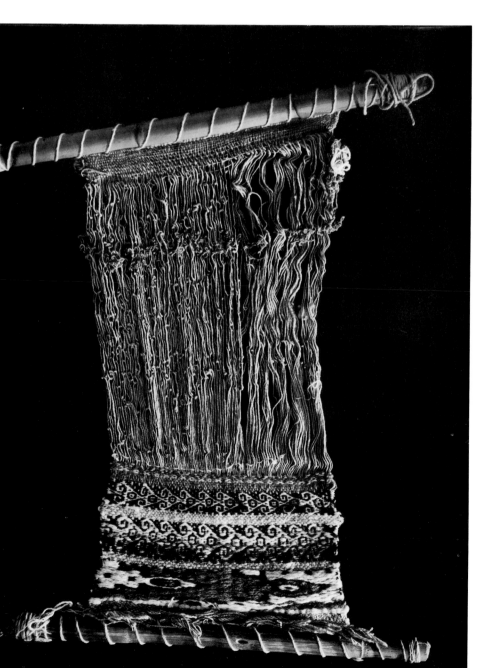

The weaving of samplers is a good way to try out ideas. A very small frame— maybe 8 by 12 inches—is convenient for this. The piece here was woven on such a frame, in this case with a continuous warp wound around both loom sticks, as shown in chapter 6, p. 77.

You will not be alone in experimenting with spacing. The Peruvian weaver who long ago was working out a design on this small loom tried out the same design in a progression of four different spacings. The results of each experiment appear very different. Many little "try-out" pieces have been found in Peru, giving us a sense of the liveliness of the weaving tradition there. This is brocade weaving, which we will explore in chapter 11. (The Peabody Museum of Archaeology and Ethnology. Photograph by Hillel Burger)

Another Way To Play with Stripes

When two colors of yarn are used alternately in both the warp and the weft of a weaving, solid, crisp, narrow stripes appear in either the horizontal or the vertical direction. Look at the reverse side of such cloth and you see the stripes running in the other direction! You can turn vertical stripes into horizontal ones on the same side of the cloth by a procedure analogous to that u by a person in a parade who finds himself out of step and double steps with one foot to exchange feet. Two consecutive rows woven with yarn of the same color will exchange vertical stripes for horizontal ones. Since this works whether the two rows are warp or weft yarns, this interesting striped weave can be woven in blocks.

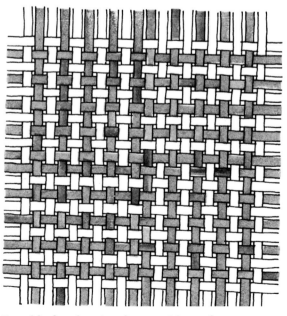

Another kind of striped cloth.

This Nigerian cloth has been set up and woven to produce rectangles of narrow stripes. While the optical effect is that of striped ribbons interwoven, careful examination shows it to be constructed of perfectly regular plain weave with two colors of yarn.

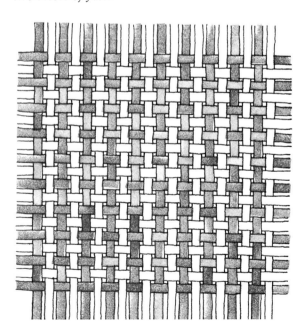

The structure of the weave shown in the striped cloth above.

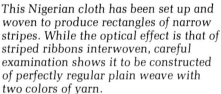

Four blocks, showing the transitions of the stripes from one direction to the other.

Another Kind of Stripe

As with all the other aspects of pattern that we have examined, some serendipitous effects follow the combination of simple elements. As an example of this, notice what happens at the crossing of two stripes, each two yarns wide: a little pinwheel appears. If two contrasting yarns separate groups of the original stripes, counter-colored pinwheels nest inside the others. The example at the right from a Guatemalan woman's skirt is of white and indigo blue.

Pinwheels at the crossing of stripes in a Guatemalan skirt.

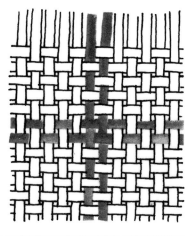

A draft of the pinwheel. While the structure of this draft is correct, the pinwheel itself is hard to see because the drawing shows the yarns with an open spacing. The cloth will need to be woven closely spaced for the pinwheel to show clearly.

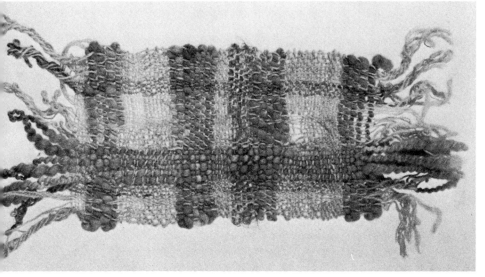

A small weaving, an experiment in using different textures of yarn.

An entirely different kind of stripe appears in this cloth from Mexico. Two yarns of contrasting color were twisted around each other before being woven through the warp. For the next pass of weft, the two yarns were twisted in the opposite direction. The result is a band of chevrons producing a stripe.

A traditional pattern for a band, found in many parts of the world.

A striped, patterned apron from Szechwan province, China. Constructed of two eight-inch bands sewn together, this brightly colored apron with its twisted fringe is all of plain-weave, warp-faced patterns, easily woven once the warp is organized. (The Peabody Museum of Archaeology and Ethnology. Photograph by Hillel Burger)

Quiet, simple stripes on an Ainu sash from Japan. (The Peabody Museum of Archaeology and Ethnology. Photograph by Hillel Burger)

8. Warp-faced Pattern

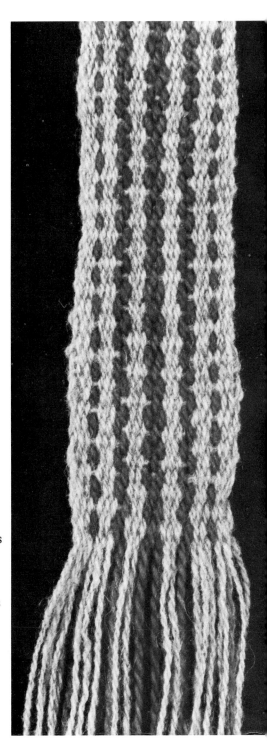

Traditional patterns for warp-faced weaving are found all over the world. Generally, they fall into two broad categories: those where warp yarns are arranged in the appropriate sequence and the pattern appears in the normal course of weaving, and those where the yarns must be specially manipulated, usually by hand in the course of weaving the cloth, as you are able to see in the traditional band on page 38. Some hints about that kind of weaving are to be found in chapter 11, on brocade weaving; the first kind will be explored in this chapter.

Similar warp-faced patterns of this sort often come from places far apart: a pattern such as that at the top right on the facing page could have been woven in many different cultures. This has happened not because the weavers were copying from each other, but because they were independently exploring the possibilities of similar structures. If you were to rediscover an old pattern while trying out various arrangements of your own yarns, you might suspect that that had occurred before and that it, too, was part of the tradition of weaving folk.

Three Threads

Many typical patterns that appear on belts, bands, or ribbons depend only upon the sequence of colored yarns in the warps for their effect. Once the warp yarns are arranged in the desired order, all that is required is to weave the band in the usual way, using whatever heddle machinery for plain weave is convenient, and the pattern appears. If one dark thread is inserted in the center of a group of pale warps, the pattern will be a dotted line; the dark thread will appear on the surface of the weaving as the sheds alternate. With two adjacent dark threads, an undulating line appears; with three threads, a stripe of a different rhythm. It seems surprising that something as simple as one, two, three can produce effects as rich and pleasing as those that do appear. Something more than mere repetition has been created.

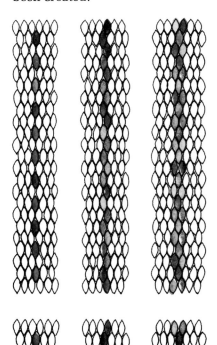

Pattern drafts show the effect made by having, from left to right, one, two, or three contrasting yarns in a warp-faced weaving. These drawings of warp-faced structures show no weft yarns at all; the warps appear vertically, as you would see them while weaving. The separate drawings at the bottom show two sheds only, telling you all you need to know to understand this cloth or to duplicate it. The order and number of warps, their division into two different groups, and the placement of contrasting threads can all be read from that drawing. Some such simple representational scheme can be worked out for any repetitive weaving.

The three stripes shown in the drafts appear thus in a real weaving.

A Notebook of Traditional Warp-faced Patterns

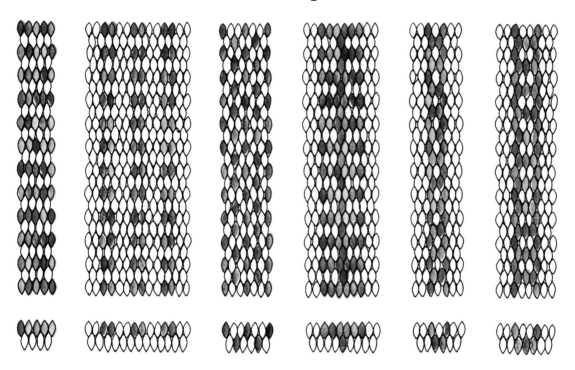

1. *The surprising crosswise stripe, made by alternating two colors in the warp.*

2. *Dots.*

3. *Different dots.*

4. *Crosswise stripes and a lengthwise stripe as well, made by combining patterns.*

5. *A simple chain.*

6. *A different chain.*

Don't be influenced by the sight of black and white in the figures to weave with two colors only: you can have the rainbow! Bands use so little yarn, their patterns are so easy to arrange, and they are woven so quickly that they become an ideal way to experiment with what happens when separate colored yarns become a single whole. Not only do you learn how a set of colors behave, you can use the product of the experiment.

All of the patterns used in warp-faced weaving can be used in weft-faced weaving as well since the structure of both types of cloth is the same. It can be impossible to tell whether a scrap of cloth, without its telltale selvedge, is warp- or weft-faced. To use any warp-faced pattern in a weft-faced cloth, use as consecutive weft yarns the colors that would have been the warps in the warp-faced pattern.

Horizontal stripes are produced in a weaving that alternates two colors of yarn as in Fig. 1.

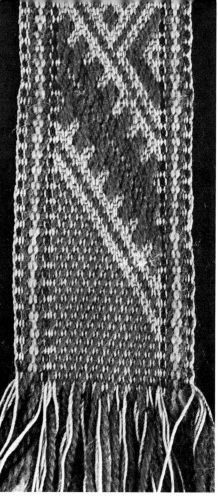

While the complex pattern in this Latvian band is difficult to weave, the pattern next to the fringe is easy to understand and weave. The warping is the same as that in Fig. 3.

A random arrangement of colors, weights and textures of yarn makes a rich surface.

After this band had been woven some distance with an alternating dark, light, dark, light arrangement of the warp, the warp was re-arranged, and the heddles restrung in an arrangement of dark, dark, light, light yarns.

Another of the traditional patterns, this one Indian.

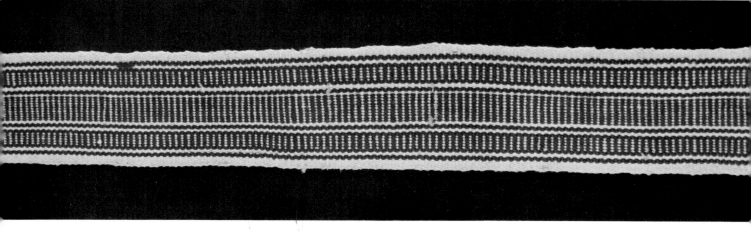

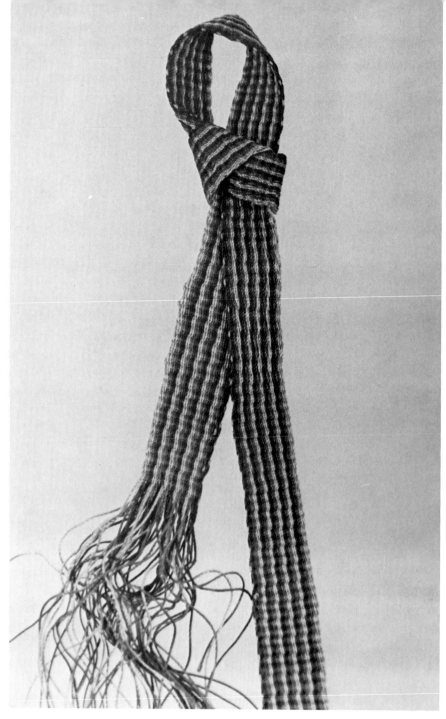

A traditional use of warp patterning: the shades of one color work their way across the band.

A narrow ribbon of silk thread.

A traditional warp-faced pattern, this one from Ireland. It is made by combining some of the patterns in this chapter.

Details of the Mexican bag in chapter 4, p. 47. Notice that warp-faced weaving doesn't have to be narrow; it can be woven as wide as your loom allows.

A traditional pattern, emphasized by using two weights of yarn, as well as two colors.

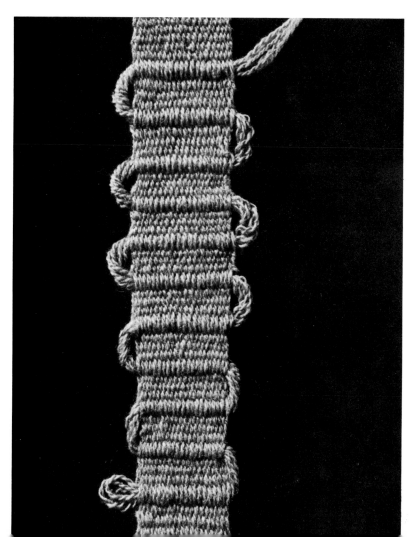

Not all warp-faced patterning need be caused by the warp yarns. Here the pattern of the weaving was made by changing the thickness of some weft yarns. This bold change of texture has a dramatic quality. The thicker yarn was made by folding the yarn used throughout into a four-yarn-thick bundle, carrying it visibly along the edge of the weaving between passes. Experiment with some thicker warp yarns too.

Ordinary twill cloth, with an unbroken diagonal structure; in the bottom part of the weaving, the light warp is crossed by a dark weft, emphasizing the diagonal effect. The top section is different only in that it has been woven with the same color yarn for warp and weft.

This little piece of Scotch tartan is woven in 2 × 2 diagonal twill, the same structure seen in the photo above. It is the traditional way to weave this cloth. The crossed stripes produce a plaid in twill as well as in plain weave. Dissecting a scrap of this sort will give you some insight into the structure of twill.

9. Twill

The patterns we have explored so far have been produced by the substitution of one thread for another, the new one differing from the old in some visible manner. The interlacement of threads has remained that of plain weave, whether the result was warp- or weft-faced or balanced. Quite different interlacements are possible that change the very structure of the cloth as well as its appearance. Exploration of these possibilities is far older than the weaving of cloth on looms: the earliest basketmakers had discovered many of the complex structural patterns still being used in many textiles, products both of the hand and of the machine.

It is characteristic in such weaves for yarns to pass over and under more than one yarn at a time. "Twill" weaves, with their diagonal bands, are typical and elegant examples, discovered within many cultures and capable of showing many variations. The word *twill* seems to be related to words that mean "two." It is an old word, probably a Scandinavian one. The specialized words weavers use hold hints of the origins and spread of textile processes. For instance, *warp* and *weft* are Anglo-Saxon; *bandanna* and *calico* are from East India; *gingham* is Malaysian, *damask* Italian, and *ikat* Indonesian. As we have used and brought together the words, so with the weaving ideas behind them.

To understand twill structure, look at it carefully and perhaps dissect a scrap of twill-woven cloth. Copy a twill draft, weaving a little sample without the help of heddles, working a needle or a stick over and under the warps. Try using two colors of yarn, one for the warp and another for the weft.

Given the same yarns, twill tends to make a slightly thicker fabric than does plain weave. The yarns are not held apart sideways by as many crossings from surface to surface of the cloth as in plain weave, and more air is trapped in the spaces: the warp's natural spacing is a little narrower than plain weave woven with the same yarns. As a result, you will often notice twill being used where warmth is wanted, especially in blankets and coatings. As a structure full of interest for the eye, it is also used for its decorative potential.

A draft for diagonal 2 × 2 twill, the simplest member of the twill family. The diagonal can slant in either direction; if it slants one way on the front of the fabric, the reverse side will show the opposite slant.

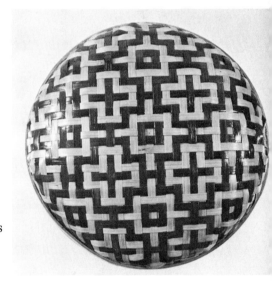

A Chinese basket in which some elements pass over and under more than one of the others at a time.

The Way To Twill

It's all very well to pick up individual warps with a needle in order to understand these weaves, but it would be enormously time-consuming to weave whole fabrics in that manner. Obviously some mechanism to open the necessary sheds would be helpful. It must permit the opening of more than two sheds, for two are not enough to produce the structure of twill. When heddles were first discovered, ways must have been found relatively quickly to organize more than two of them, thus permitting more variety in the structures of the woven cloth. After all, those more complex structures had already been known and used by generation after generation of basketweavers who used no other machinery than their hands.

The stick and string heddles shown in chapter 6 are representative of a very old type. While using them you probably noticed that you were limited to only one stick heddle, which had to be the heddle farthest from the active edge of the weaving. While the stick heddle does have that limitation, there is the possibility of more than one string heddle: string heddles permit a shed from behind them to "pass through." In fact, you can have as many string heddles as you wish (examine the saddle blanket, p. 80). But how many do you need, and how should they be organized?

In twill weaving, two general, traditional solutions have been used. If you analyze a 2x2 twill, you will see that there are four different weft paths in the cloth: any weft crossing from one edge of the cloth to the other edge follows one of these four paths. You can consider the warps which the wefts pass under as the yarns needing to be picked up in turn by four sets of heddles: three string heddles, and the fourth, the stick heddle, at the back of the loom. It turns out that every warp is picked up twice, by two different heddles, since every warp appears on two different paths. This arrangement works perfectly well: you weave the twill by first lifting heddle 1, then 2, 3, 4, and back to 1. If you want to change the direction of the twill diagonal, you can do so by reversing the order in which you lift the heddles to 4, 3, 2, 1, 4, etc.

The other solution to the heddle problem is even more elegant, requiring each warp to be attached to only one heddle, thus saving preparation time. Notice that the four weft paths require four different *sheds*, but that you can lift more than one heddle to make a shed. In the photo, two heddles are being lifted at once, together making one of the twill sheds. The beater has been inserted in that shed, and the shuttle will be able to pass through. If more than one heddle will be raised to make a shed, how do you choose which yarns to attach to each heddle? Some study of the drawings on this page or some experimentation on a sampler warp might provide you with an answer for yourself.

One way is to choose those warps that are not held down by a weft crossing them when you look at the possible weft paths in pairs. In Figure B a pair of paths is shown: only three warps—the fourth, eighth, and twelfth—are free of crossings by weft yarns. Attach those to the first heddle. Pair the second and third paths (fig. C) to choose warps for the next heddle; then pair the third and fourth paths, and finally the fourth and first. That gives you four heddles, each with one quarter of the warps attached to it. Now if you lift heddles 1 and 2 together, you will be opening your first twill shed. To weave a diagonal twill, the order for lifting heddles is 1 and 2, 2 and 3, 3 and 4, 4 and 1, or vice versa. That is the way the Navaho weaver on page 64 has set up her loom for weaving the twill blanket.

This arrangement of heddles permits many other sheds to be opened, depending on how many and which heddles are lifted simultaneously. Since the order in which the sheds are made can also be changed, much more than 2x2 diagonal twill can be woven with heddles set up in this way. Spend some time experimenting with the possibilities: some of the combinations will surprise you. Either of the two general schemes presented here for arranging your heddles will work for any twill weave: both have been used since antiquity. The first takes extra time to set up; the second, extra time to figure out.

As you weave along, you'll notice that the edges of a twill weaving don't behave as regularly as those of plain weave. If you send the weft back and forth without paying attention to what goes on at the edges, you will soon realize that they are quite uneven and have loops of uncaught warps every so often. While you can never make the edges of twill look as smooth as those of plain weave, you can partially remedy the situation by hand

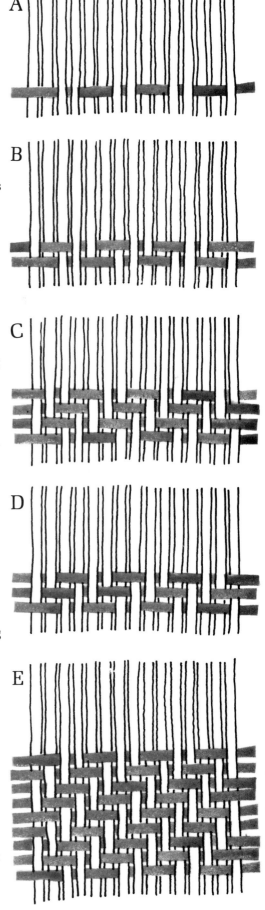

A

B

C

D

E

The drafts here show the four paths the weft takes to produce a 2 × 2 twill, the yarn passing under and over two warps at a time. A different shed opening is needed for each of those paths. The final drawing shows the cloth; built up by repetitions of the four weft journeys.

manipulation at your edges: send the heddle around warp yarns that would be left outside of the weaving for several rows and the selvedge will be smoother. The Kashmir scarf on p. 82 shows that even the most expert weaver cannot make a perfectly smooth edge on twill.

It is possible to weave any twill pattern as either a warp- or weft-faced cloth: those are spacing relationships not affected by the structural requirements of twills. Spread the warps and beat harder to make the weft predominate; crowd the warp yarns for the opposite effect. What appears may not be what you expected, but that is no reason not to explore what might happen.

A loom set up with four heddles to weave twill. Three of the heddles carry string loops; the fourth heddle is a stick inserted into the shed. This loom has a long warp wrapped around it.

Herringbone Twill

Diagonal 2x2 twill is only the simplest member of a large family. Consider some variations: if, while weaving, you change the direction of the diagonal, you produce the "herringbone" design. To do this you need only reverse the order in which you lift the heddles: each time you reverse, the direction of the diagonal changes. The effect is very different if you change that direction often or seldom. Or, you could weave for quite a while sending the diagonal in one direction and then step only a little in the other direction, making a different design. There are many other ideas to explore.

If you examine any cloth of herringbone twill carefully, you will see that the warp does not go over and under all of the wefts by twos. Near the places where the zigzags occur, the warp passes across three, or even sometimes even one, weft yarns. This happens without control on the weaver's part; it is a necessary consequence of the relationships of the yarns.

Herringbone twill, using a light warp and a dark weft. This is an example of an evenly stepped twill.

Diamond Twill

In the herringbone twill just discussed the pattern changes across a horizontal line. For the twill diagonal to change across a vertical line, a different strategy is needed. The horizontal change is made by a symmetrical reversal of the order in which the *sheds* are opened; the vertical change can be made by a symmetrical reversal of *the order in which the warps are attached to their heddles*. To set up for this, you can either start to arrange your heddles as for a regular diagonal twill and reverse the order of tying up where you choose, or you can copy a draft for a herringbone pattern. When you weave this pattern, the zigzag rows will look exactly like the other herringbone turned sideways.

This may seem like a lot of work to invest in an effect that can be had without organizing a new arrangement of heddles, but there is a reward for the effort. If you now also reverse the order in which you raise the heddles, the opening V's of the herringbone will close up, their diagonals changing direction, and become interlocked diamonds! These can be manipulated to be big or small, nested inside each other, or left open in meandering lines.

The diamond twill pattern, like many others, has been found and used by people all over the world. If you are newly a weaver, you will be particularly able to appreciate the qualities of thought, acute observation, memory, and skill that the weavers who discovered this pattern long ago must have had. Twill is an ancient triumph of the weaver's art.

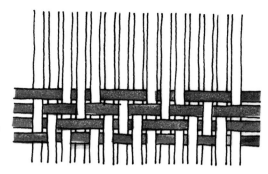

A draft for either a "sideways" herringbone twill or a diamond twill. Here are the four paths needed to make the pattern.

the sideways herringbone twill draft. Notice the breaks in the 2 × 2 pattern. The reverse side of a diamond twill looks similar, but is not exactly the same as the first side.

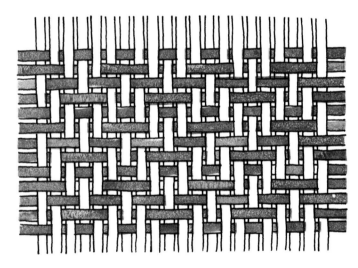

The pattern as it appears when the four weft paths are repeated in turn.

Evenly stepped herringbone twill.

Diamond twill. This weave is often
called "goose-eye."

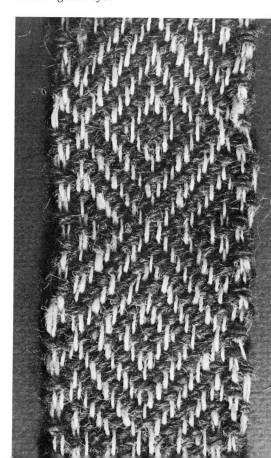

A long cotton scarf from Burma. This
bright piece, woven in blue, red, and
yellow yarns takes advantage of the
weaver's ability to change from
herringbone to diamond twill at will.
(The Peabody Museum of Archaeology
and Ethnology. Photograph by Hillel
Burger)

2x2 Twill Variations

Colored yarns interspersed in the background color of a twill will produce stripes, as the tartan on page 96 shows. Some other special striped effects are possible with twills. The draft (right) is a 2×2 diagonal twill, the heddles set up in the regular way. Both the warp and the weft alternate two dark with two light yarns, yet the cloth shows vertical stripes. What appears on the reverse side?

Another variation of twill that requires no change in the regular heddle arrangement is the checkered pattern called hound's tooth. It is related to the little pinwheel shown on p. 89. Experiment with different stripe widths; you can make many effects.

A draft for an interesting twill stripe.

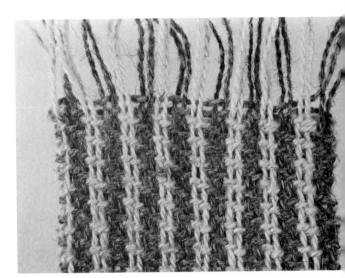

A sample of cloth woven from the draft above.

A draft of hound's tooth check with the colored yarns alternating in groups of four. The draft shows the structure of this cloth to be ordinary 2×2 diagonal twill, changed only by the addition of color.

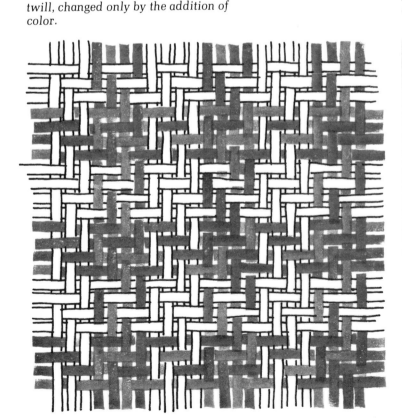

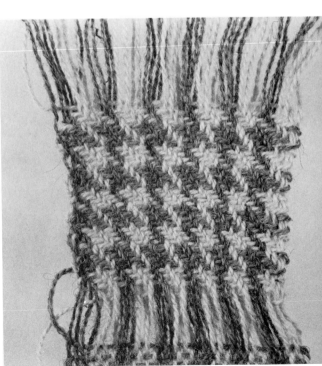

Cloth woven from the draft to the left.

Uneven Twills

Twill cloth can have many possible structures other than 2x2. When the yarns in a twill pass over a different number of yarns than they go under, the weave is called "uneven," and the resulting cloth looks different. Blue denim, with a 2x1 interlacement, is a ubiquitous example of this. The warp yarns of denim are blue, the wefts are white. The outside of jeans appears predominantly blue because the warps cross over two and under one weft, while on the inside, it is the wefts that pass over two yarns.

The relationships of the yarns in weaving are restricted by many unexpected bits of orderliness. If you experimentally needle-weave wefts into a warp choosing any irregular over-under path, stepping the rows of weaving along in the diagonal array of twill, then the warps turn out to have that same numerical relationship, too, regardless of what intentions the weaver may have had. If you weave your weft over three and under two, that is how the warps will appear on the other side of the cloth. The same holds true if your path is made of equal steps as well, except it doesn't then seem so surprising.

Uneven twills are interesting to play around with. They can result in herringbones, diamonds, checks, all the variations that are possible with the more regular twills, but they will look quite different. You may have already discovered some of these effects if you experimented with other possibilities for sheds when you first wove 2x2 twill, earlier in this chapter.

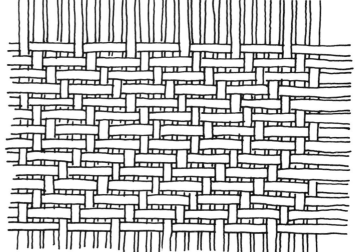

Denim cloth has a 2 × 1 twill weave with blue warps, white wefts. Taking a scrap of this apart carefully will show you its structure. If you try to weave it, you will discover it needs only three heddles.

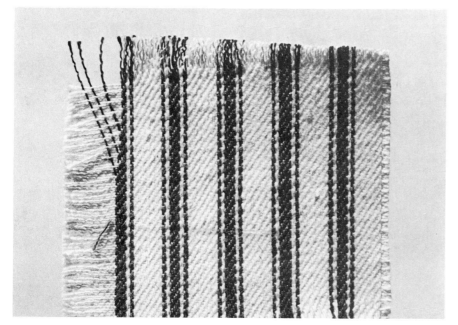

Mattress ticking is woven with a 3 × 1 twill pattern.

A 3 × 1 twill, with a herringbone reversal.

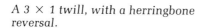

A loose flowing garment from Oaxaca, Mexico. The three panels that are sewn together to make this huipil alternate bands of gauze weave with bands of plain weave. The center panel has the added embellishment of brocade. This is by no means a grand piece: the workmanship shows it to have been woven in haste, yet its very unevenness seems lively and full of interest.

Four partial rows of gauze weave decorate a plain weave shirt in a bold scale. (Piece woven by Lillian Ball)

10. Holes

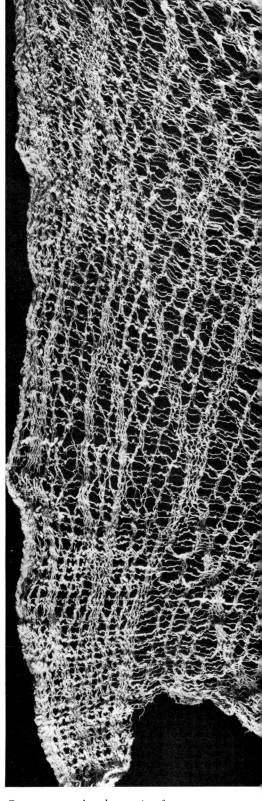

The space left between the yarns of a weaving are holes, as we saw in chapter 7, but far more decorative, useful, and interesting holes can be deliberately woven. Two ways to weave holes are presented here. Weaves full of open space, permitting the motion of air, seem to be found most often in warm climates, whereas the twill weaves seemed especially useful to folk in need of warmth. Holes can let you see what is beyond the fabric, as curtains at a window, or they can have work to perform, as when a hole joins with a button to hold something together. Added to all of that, holes in themselves are used to add interest to the appearance of textiles.

Gauze

Gauze is an extraordinary weave in which the warp yarns are not independent of each other, but are distorted sideways, crossing each other, and are held in their new positions by the weft. One might weave for a long time and never discover these curious relationships of yarn to yarn. Indeed, only some weaving cultures ever used this technique: it has been found in old weaving only in the Americas and eastern Asia. Wonderful examples have been excavated from archaeological sites in Peru, and it is still being woven on back-strap looms in Guatemala and Mexico today.

The crossing of the warp threads in gauze weave prevents the weft threads from being beaten back tightly, so openings in the web occur, although the weave can be made relatively dense. Those warp crossings also keep the wefts from sliding around, allowing extremely open and flimsy cloth that retains its form. The gauzy Peruvian head-covering and the loose-flowing garment shown here exemplify these extremes.

Cloth can be woven entirely of gauze weave, of gauze bands alternating with bands of other weaves, or of a single row of gauze in a field of something else; each makes its own effect and each is interesting. In fact, nothing requires that a whole row of weaving be gauze: you can weave just a part of any row in gauze where you wish, making a little strip or building up to a planned shape over several rows. The different texture of the open-work related to the background weave is quite noticeable.

Gauze-woven head covering from pre-Columbian Peru. When this weave is woven loosely, as it is here, the aptness of its name becomes perfectly clear. This piece is entirely of gauze weave, but two interlacements are used, one a little denser than the other, forming the shadowy diamond pattern. (The Peabody Museum of Archaeology and Ethnology. Photograph by Hillel Burger)

To Weave Gauze

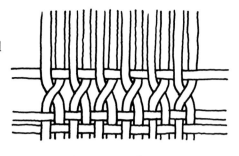

If you are making only a row or two of gauze crossings, it is easy to do it all by manipulations of the warp threads with your fingers and a beater or a weaver's pick like the one shown in the Appendix on Tools. The simplest example of this weave has a one-over-one crossing. Figures 1-4 give the steps in weaving gauze. First weave a plain weave shed. Using your fingers, and beginning at the right selvedge, cross one of each pair of warp threads over the other. (In each pair of warp threads, one will lie behind the just-woven weft: that is the warp that should cross above the other one.) Enter the beater to secure that crossing. Do the same across the row, then turn the beater on edge and weave the weft across. You will see that the crossings will prevent you from beating back too tightly, producing holes. Now weave the same plain weave shed as the one you wove before, and your warp will automatically "uncross"! Alternating these two rows will make a cloth all of gauze. However, one row of gauze, or even a partial row, can be a beautiful effect in itself. As you weave along, take care that the tension on your warp does not become too great. The extra distance the warp thread travels on its undulating path means you must loosen the warp tension more often.

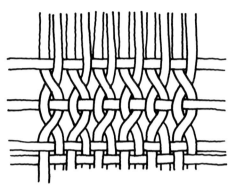

Two drafts showing the structure of gauze. At the top, the gauze crosses have been made and are held with a row of weft. At the bottom, the proper plain weave shed has been opened, forcing the warps to "uncross"; the new weft is in place.

A fine bast fiber cloth from Japan, with partial rows of gauze weave building up a pattern by the subtle change of texture.

1. Beginning to cross the warps.

3. The weft yarn now holds the gauze crosses in place.

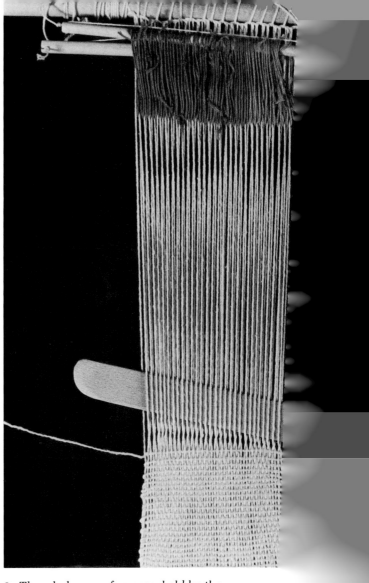

2. The whole row of crosses, held by the beater.

4. The plain weave shed has been woven.

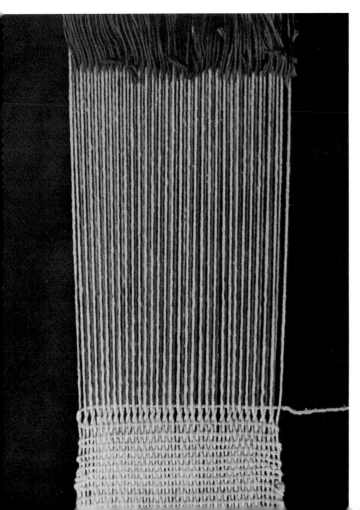

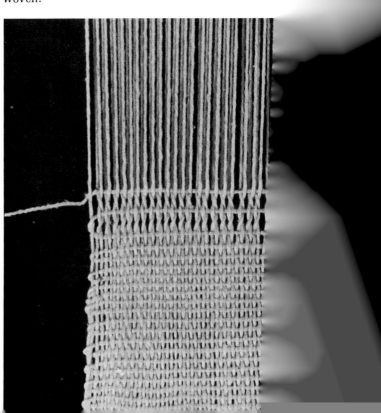

The diagonal distortions of gauze can be emphasized by sending a weft yarn over or under more than one warp before holding the crossings in place with a weft. The effect of this is very different; a structure of this family appears in the Peruvian gauze on p. 105. Extra wefts can weave in-and-out between those that hold the crosses; they add to the visual effect, but are not structurally required.

If you are making many rows of crossings, you may want to have the crossed shed open automatically, instead of having to cross each warp pair with your fingers. That is easy to do with string heddles. Make the first crossing row by hand, entering your beater to hold it. Pick up each of the warps that lie on top of the beater with a string-heddle loop as in chapter 6, arranging the loops on their own heddle stick. This shed will open a little oddly, since it will pull the warps sideways under other warps before it pulls them up, but it will open none the less.

Since the loom you are using is very like the looms used by the women who invented gauze cloth, it's not surprising that the machinery works so easily to help you to weave it. It's much harder to make a modern frame loom with wire heddles and foot-operated treadles do this old trick.

The diagonal distortions of gauze can be emphasized by sending a warp yarn over or under more than one warp before holding the crossings in place with a weft. The effect of this is very different; a structure of this family appears in the gauze-woven head-covering shown at the beginning of this chapter. Extra wefts can weave in-and-out between those that hold the crosses; they add to the visual effect, but are not required for the structure.

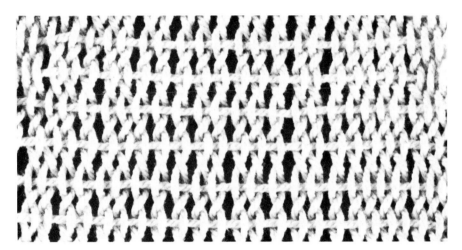

Gauze weave made by alternating a crossing row and a plain weave row. Notice that the same warp thread is always the upper one at the crossings and that the warp yarns don't go around each other.

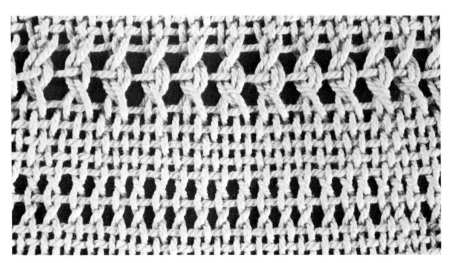

Many different crossings are possible with gauze weave. Here is a row of one-over-one and also a row of two-over-two gauze. You can find many beautiful effects if you experiment for yourself.

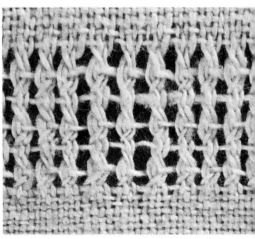

A detail of the Mexican huipil shown earlier in this chapter. Notice the softly twisted, fuzzy, hand-spun cotton yarn.

Another gauze from ancient Peru, producing an entirely different effect from the loosely woven head covering shown at the beginning of this chapter. The cloth here was woven entirely of one-over-one gauze crossings. The stripes, waves, and birds were woven over those gauze pairs, using them as a scaffolding, in a kind of brocade. (The Peabody Museum of Archaeology and Ethnology. Photograph by Hillel Burger)

A detail of the ancient Peruvian gauze, shown above.

Slits

An entirely different way to make woven holes is to weave slits—either functional or ornamental. The slits that appear in the weft-faced slit-woven band from Peru shown here are decorative, while the slit across the stomach of the tigre in the serape was intended as a head-hole. In this case the weaver sewed the hole closed temporarily. Slits can be long or short, few or many in a weaving, but they must run in the same direction as do the warp yarns.

To weave slits, you will need to prepare two shuttles: at the desired place in the weaving, begin to weave with both of them, one for each half of the warp, as though you were making two weavings on the same loom. If you let one side of the weaving run ahead of the other it may be hard to beat the weaving back evenly. When the opening has become as long as you want, the right size for a button or for a head, drop one shuttle and weave on across the whole warp as before. Your slit is completed.

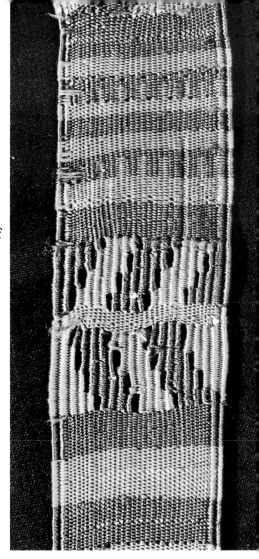

A decorative slit-woven band from Peru.

A narrow band from Guatemala, a design unusual in that this narrow weaving is weft-faced. The pattern in the middle of the band has slits woven in it.

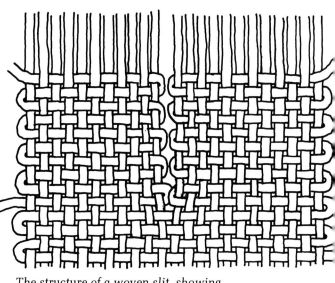

The structure of a woven slit, showing the two weft yarns needed. The slit is parallel to the warps.

A serape from Oaxaca, Mexico.

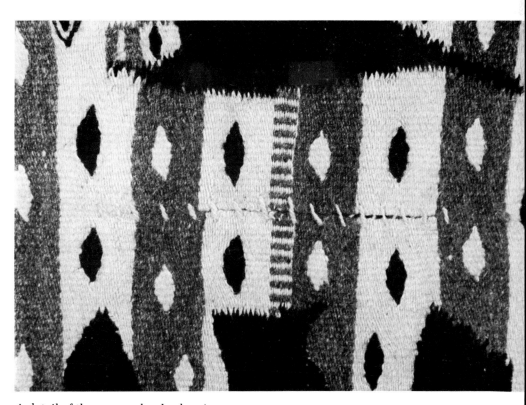

A detail of the serape clearly showing
the slit.

Variations

Although it looks quite different, the same method of making slits is used in the cloth from tropical Nigeria shown here. The four-inch wide band has a surface of extra threads carried on one side of the cloth, as well as rows of holes that are really distorted slits. The many diagonal threads that are carried loosely across the surface of this weaving become the weft threads only in the small areas between individual slits. The slits appear different from the ones we have been examining: they are rounder. That is because the warps are distorted by the three rows of weaving at the slits. A single weft yarn weaves the plain weave areas for the rest of the band. Looking at such cloth from one side, only the slits decorate the material, while on the reverse side the extra weft threads are carried across the surface from hole to hole, adding another texture to the cloth. Eleven strips such as this, sewn together, make a woman's wrapped dress.

A contemporary tapestry woven of layers of slits. (The work of Libby Buskirk)

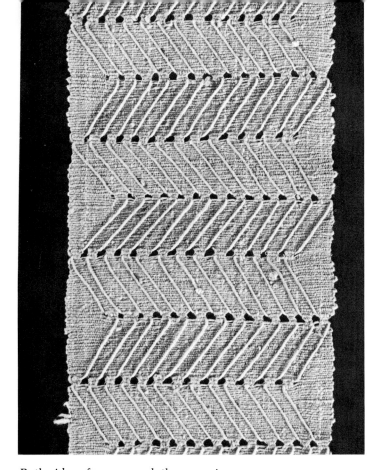
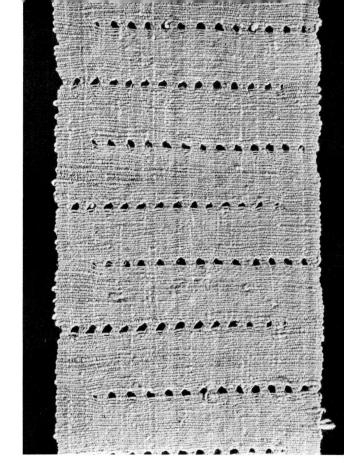

Both sides of a narrow cloth woven in
Ilesha, Nigeria.

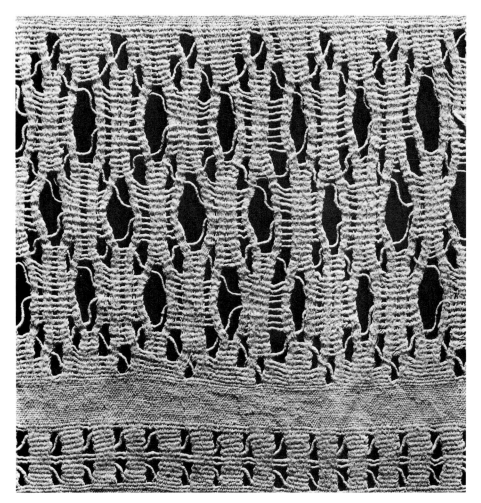

These slits are similar to those in the
Nigerian band, but only a single weft
thread works its way across the series of
holes, most easily understood by
studying the row of slits at the bottom of
this figure. This cloth is from Spain, and
the technique is called "Spanish lace."
(The Museum of Fine Arts, Boston)

A Western Nigerian strip weaving with brocade embellishments. The dark blue pattern is on hand-spun beige cotton.

Another African strip weaving, this one the famous Kente cloth from Ghana, of gold, blue, red, and green yarns, with several different areas of brocade. When many strips are sewn together, the effect is dazzling.

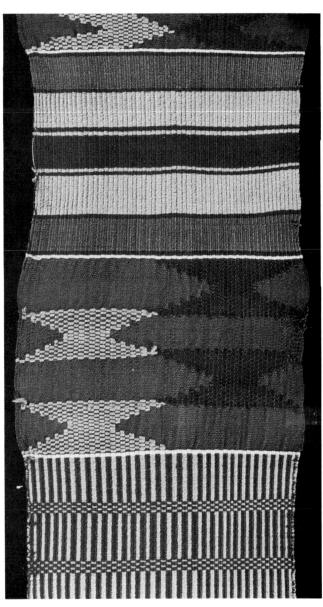

The simplest loom provides the necessary freedom for the most complex weaving. Here, a Mexican backstrap loom, with stick and string heddles providing the sheds for plain weave, has had its central panel decorated with brocade patterns. The pattern weaving was hand-manipulated. This is the same loom as that on page 80. (You can see the position of the stretcher bar, held in place with thorns, just where the weaving ends.)

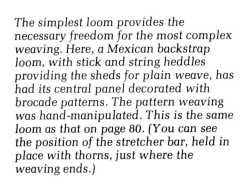

11. Brocade: Weaving between the Lines

A clothing label woven in brocade. The labels are woven as long ribbons, repeating the symbolic information every few inches; the warp yarns are therefore horizontal in this figure.

Two kinds of labels are sewn into clothing: printed ones and woven ones. If you look carefully at one of the woven kind, you will see that the design is made by threads that lie on top of the cloth of the label for a distance, then pass through that cloth, and lie under until they are needed on top again. You could imagine that the threads were embroidered after the cloth had been woven, but that is not so. The pattern threads are woven into the warp of the cloth between each shed of the plain weave, which itself provides the structure of the cloth. Look through your closet for clothing labels and examine them closely. This type of weaving is called "brocade."

Many degrees of freedom are possible with this technique. The weft yarns can slip in and out of the base cloth at will, allowing shaped designs of every sort. The pattern threads do not have to provide the structural integrity of the final textile; colors and yarns can be changed at any time, even within single rows of weaving. Yarns, thick or thin, can be used together to blend color or texture; the brocade yarns can be displayed boldly, with only an occasional warp yarn crossing them. With this weave, curving "organic" forms, as well as the geometric forms traditional to it, can be made.

Any structure so versatile will have been used by many weavers; examination of old weavings bears this out: brocade weaving is found everywhere. In some places—West Africa is one—brocade seems to be the typical way to embellish cloth.

Weaving Brocade

Begin by weaving a sampler so that you are free to explore the mechanics of this weave, especially the effects produced by the relative weights of pattern and background yarns. Set up a loom to weave balanced plain-weave of a relatively open structure. Have the first yarn you will use for brocading be thicker than the background yarns. It could be made of several thinner yarns used as one, allowing you easily to vary its thickness by changing the number of yarns. The background weft will be the same as the warp yarn and will use the alternating plain-weave sheds made by the regular machinery of your loom.

Between these weft yarns will lie the brocade yarn, making a pattern by appearing and disappearing. Use your beater and, either by eye or by counting warp threads, find and open the shed for the brocade yarn. After you have made the first weft pass of brocade thread, it is usually easy to see without counting what path you need for the next pattern weft. Alternate your plain-weave sheds between the pattern ones. The plain-weave is like a simple rhythmic chord sequence supporting a melody. Once you have the hang of it, the rhythm of the work will carry you on.

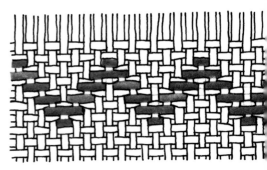

A drawing of the structure of brocade. For clearness, the pattern wefts are not drawn where they pass behind the background weave.

A brocade sampler, part of which follows the drawing above.

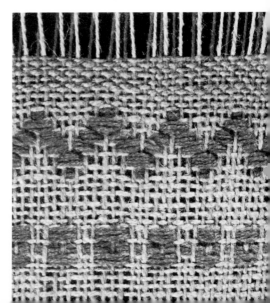

To Weave Brocade

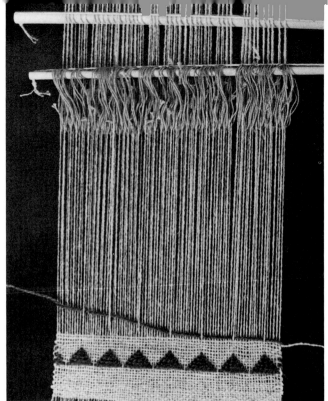

1. The brocade pattern sheds are formed "by hand." Use your usual beater or one with a more delicate point to find the sheds. This figure shows the brocade shed being picked up. Eleven threads have been skipped for every one chosen. The young weaver on page 66 is finding the sheds to weave her brocade pattern.

2. The pattern yarn is in that shed, which begins a repeat of the row of triangles already woven.

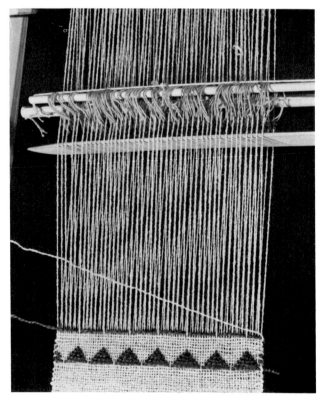

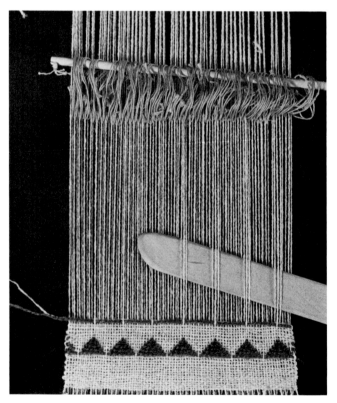

3. The next plain weave row.

4. The second brocade shed picks up three warps at the place where one was picked up before.

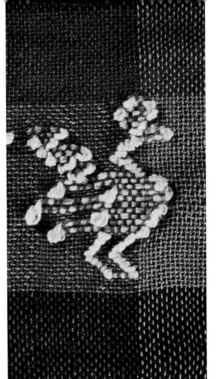

Brocade patterns can be made by a weft
yarn that passes from selvedge to
selvedge, as at the left, or one that just
goes back and forth the width of a little
design, as in the middle. At the right is
the reverse side of one of the woven
birds, showing that each bird is woven
of a single pattern yarn. The fringed
cloth is a traditional eastern European
design; the other is Mexican.

Brocade yarns can float over and under
several warps of the base cloth (right), or
can live inside the plain weave sheds
and show only by texture or color (left).
Because the second variation has no
long loose yarns, it is a better choice for
articles that will receive hard abrasive
wear. Both examples are Mexican.

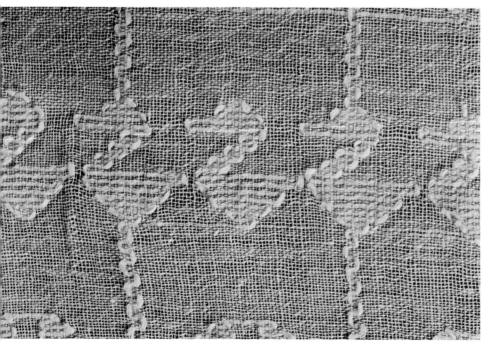

Brocade effects are not dependent upon color contrasts, although they often use them. Here the brocade yarns are made of groups of the yarn used throughout and appear as a change of texture within the very open ground weave.

Brocade is thought of as a manipulation of weft threads, but the equivalent relationships can be made as well with warp threads, floating over and under a base fabric. To weave thus, set up your warp with the pattern threads interspaced where they belong, and then manipulate them appropriately as you come to them, sending them above or below the cloth as you weave. Only patterns in which a brocade yarn extends the whole length of the cloth are suitable for this. The ribbon on the right is a traditional Scandinavian design, that on the left an experimental sampler.

More than any other pattern-making technique shown in this book, this way of weaving between the rows holds the possibility of great diversity. Until you try it for yourself, you will have only a limited idea of what can be done. Experiment freely, trying different forms, weights of yarn, spacing, and colors. Use what others have done before you as aids to learning, but do not stop where they stopped; go on to make that which is your own.

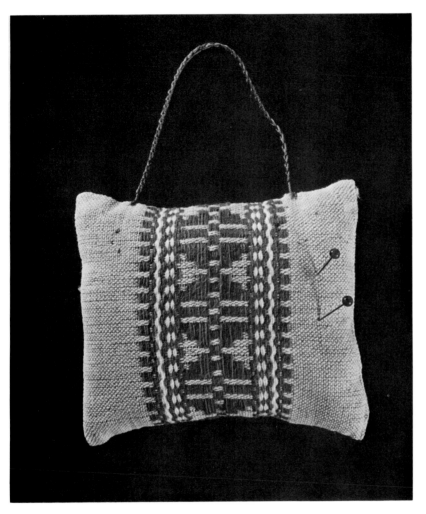

Not all that appears to be brocade is so: this Mexican pouch was embroidered with needle and thread after the background cloth was woven. The same pattern is often used as a woven one also.

Another Mexican bird.

A tiny pincushion of linen, brocaded in Switzerland.

Not all woven birds come from the New World. These roosters and castles, worked in reverse, are from Renaissance Italy. The cloth is linen, the brocade yarn is dyed with indigo. (The Museum of Fine Arts, Boston)

A garden blossoms, inlaid between the wefts. Turkish. (Ross Collection, the Museum of Fine Arts, Boston)

Postscript

Long ago in Peru, that most weaverly of places, the little dolls shown here were made by weavers. Wrapped, braided, fringed, woven with pattern of every sort, these strange figures are a statement of their maker's skills, regardless of what other enigmatic function they served. Having come to the end of this book, you too might be ready to combine your new skills: what better way than to join in this tradition and make a figure such as these shown here that is a sampler of what you can do? The doll you make might teach and inform weavers not yet born.

Dolls taken from archaeological digs at
Chancay, Peru. (Denver Art Museum)

A broken umbrella contains many big needles.

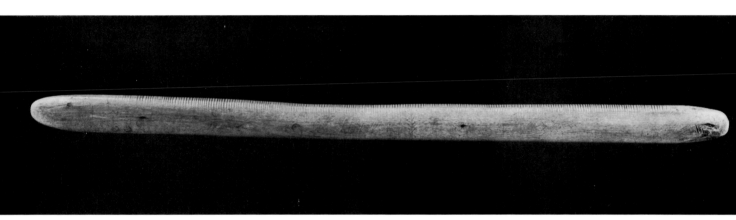

An old, worn, smooth beater, shiny from much handling. Much cloth must have been made with this tool, for the warps which it held open have left marks all along its length. Navaho. (The Peabody Museum of Archaeology and Ethnology. Photography by Hillel Burger)

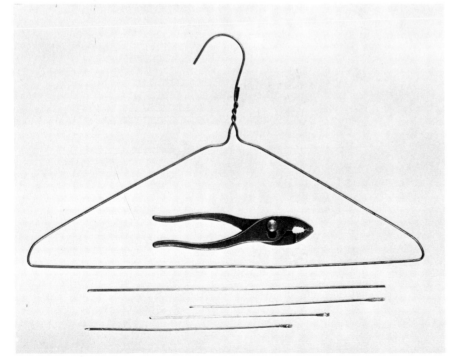

A coat hanger can be made into large needles.

Appendix: Tools

Beginners need good tools—tools that support the emerging development of new skills; tools that work well. Such tools are, more often than not, expensive. For people who are not yet certain of their commitment to a craft, or for teachers who must be thoughtful of the needs of whole groups of students, the two horns of this dilemma create a difficult problem. This book has tried to treat this problem very seriously, not only by looking at the old ways of doing things, with their time-tested solutions to the design of tools; but also with some care for the materials and skills available now to people who might make their own. The making of tools is suggested throughout the book; here are details of construction and materials to complete those suggestions.

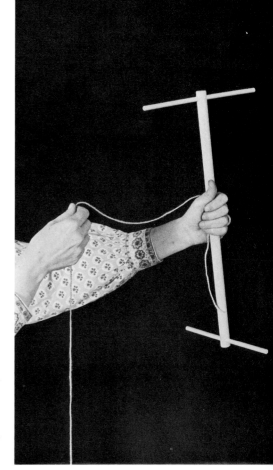

A Niddy-Noddy

Ours is made of ¾-inch and ⁵/₁₆-inch dowels. The ¾-inch shaft is 18 inches long, the cross-arms 9 inches. Drill ⁵/₁₆-inch holes near each end of the shaft, remembering to make the holes at right angles to each other. Tap the cross arms into place, glueing if necessary.

If you have no way to drill the holes, file or whittle a rounded notch for the cross-arms at each end of the shaft, and glue the cross-arms in place. In that case, the niddy-noddy will be stronger if you bind the ends with string dipped into glue.

This tool should not be given a slippery surface finish.

Skeins wound on a niddy-noddy of the dimensions given here are about two yards around.

A Scale To Weigh Yarns

Use a postage scale if you have one. If not, make this one, which you can use to weigh mail as well!

This ball of wool weighs two ounces.

Materials You Will Need

A container of cardboard or plastic. (Ours came with a quart of ice cream inside.)
String
A rubber band, medium size
A piece of cardboard
Sticky tape

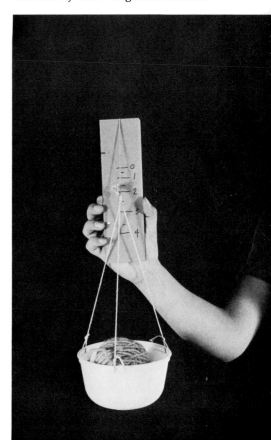

Cut the rubber band open. Poke three evenly spaced holes around the carton's rim. Attach three pieces of string to those holes. Gather the strings together at the top, adding the rubber band to the bundle and tie them together in an overhand knot. Pass the rubber band to the back of the cardboard; tape it there securely.

To calibrate the scale, mark "0 ounces" where the knot hangs in front of the cardboard when the container is empty. Add one ounce of water to the container, using a kitchen measuring cup. Remember one volume ounce of water weighs one weight ounce. Mark the knot's new position on the cardboard. Continue in the same way, marking 2, 3, and 4 ounces.

Your rubber band will eventually stretch, no longer returning to zero when the container is empty. When that happens, replace the rubber band and calibrate the new one.

Weavers' Long Needles

Long needles, sometimes called baling needles, are sold by many weavers' suppliers, but it is very satisfying to make your own. A rib of a defunct umbrella makes a fine needle, traditionally used by weavers the world over. Each rib comes complete with an eye. All that's needed to transform it is to cut it to the length you wish and smooth the cut end. That can be done by rubbing it on a rock, a sidewalk, or on sandpaper.

The ubiquitous wire coat hanger can be transformed into splendid needles. Cut straight pieces to the lengths you wish. Even a common household plier will make the cuts if you bear down when the wire is in the notch nearest the plier's pivot. Hammer one end of the wire flat. You'll need a sturdy flat surface to hammer on—the anvil part of a vise or a piece of scrap metal. As you beat on the wire, it will flatten and broaden. Use as few blows as possible, to keep the metal of the wire from becoming too brittle.

Drill a hole in the flattened portion: an egg-beater drill does this job well. Make a little dimple at the exact point you want the hole to be, using a center punch or a nail. This keeps the drill from skittering around before the hole starts forming. Shape and smooth the point of your needle by grinding it on a stone or sandpaper. Making tools of metal is an art much younger than that of weaving cloth.

Beaters and Shuttles

If you look at old looms in museums, you will notice that the beaters are the most beautiful parts of the mechanisms: the hands and the yarns of the weavers have worn them to a smooth finish, their shapes have been refined by their use. For your own, certainly start with what comes to hand, tools like the ruler-beater and the cardboard shuttle, which let you get started right away. But remain on the lookout for the tools you too will cherish.

Sometimes you are lucky enough to come upon tools used by weavers before you; sometimes you can adapt a tool used for another purpose. If you start with material that's already part-way there, you'll need little in the way of tools to make your tools. Saws cut wood, of course, but so do knives; if the cut's not too large, even a serrated bread knife can manage it. Or you can invest in just the blade of a hack saw, wrapping it for part of its length to make a handle. Files shape and smooth wood, but so do stones, and sandpaper, and even nail files.

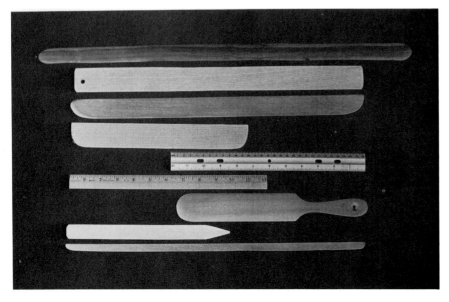

Beaters (from top to bottom): A Navaho shed stick—the Navaho weaver beats her weft with a comb-shaped tool, using this long stick to hold her shed open while she passes the weft through it; a beautiful thin, tapered slat of strong wood, the batten from a sail, available at boat supply stores—a piece of sandpaper will transform it, smoothing and shaping its end; another batten, become a beater; a piece of lath from the lumber yard, filed but not yet tapered; a plastic ruler; a wooden ruler without a metal ferrule—sandpapering is all it needs; a kitchen tool, useful as is; a garden stake needs some shaping; a slender beater is useful near the end of a weaving—it could have a hole drilled in it to double as a needle.

Shape your beaters and shuttles, using your understanding of what those shapes should be, smooth them, and use them. About sizes: beaters need to be longer than your weaving is wide; shuttles can be shorter than that. Beaters, when turned on edge, should open the shed enough for the shuttle to pass through easily. Both tools should be flat.

Loom Sticks, Heddle Sticks, Stretcher Sticks

The sticks you gather yourself in the woods will give you more pleasure than any others. You will come to know the trees they come from as well. Choose sticks to be strong, not snapping if bent a bit. Different thicknesses, varying as the fingers of your hand, are useful. Choose pieces that are straight for the lengths you'll need.

Wooden dowels can be found in hardware stores as well as in lumber yards. When you come to buy them, look them over and choose ones with handsome grain and color. If you plan ahead, you can take advantage of the fact that they come in 36-inch lengths, as well as many diameters. When their use is as loom sticks, they need to be rigid enough not to be deflected by the tension on the warp. For weavings of moderate width, ½ - inch dowels are fine. Wider weavings might need ⅝ -inch or ¾ -inch ones. Look at the photographs in chapter 6 to judge what you need. Half-inch diameter dowels—or even smaller—will do for heddle sticks, too. After a while, you'll have accumulated a variety of sizes. Any small saw, even a hacksaw blade without its frame, will cut sticks and dowels. Sand the cut edges smooth, but don't finish the cylindrical surfaces in a way that would make them slippery.

Frames

Frames should be strong enough to withstand the tensions placed on them by your weavings. Old picture frames can be fine if they're sturdy. Artists' canvas stretcher strips work very well. They are very inexpensive, and they come apart for easy storage. Art supply shops, some fabric stores, even department stores carry them. You'll need to buy four strips, in two pairs, for your first loom: perhaps two 18-inch and two 24-inch pieces. A pair of 36-inch pieces added to these would permit you to assemble an alternate larger loom, or a pair of 14-inch ones would let you make a smaller frame. No tools are required for assembly or disassembly. Just push the corners together. See chapter 6.

Storage

In the southwestern United States, many weavers store their weaving tools in a bag made of a leg from a pair of blue-jeans sewn closed. You could make this "traditional" tool if you wished.

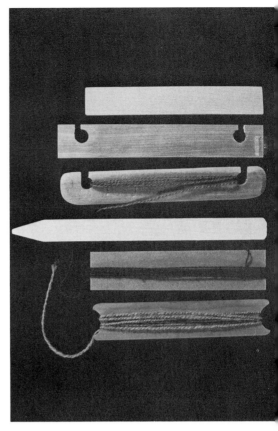

Shuttles need not be elaborate. You will be repaid in pleasure and pride by the care you take with the simple task of making them.

Mail-Order Resources

The mails are a powerful way to reach out farther than your local suppliers. You will find that some places charge you for their catalog and their yarn samples: they are usually well worth the cost.

Suppliers of Tools, Yarns, Books, Looms

Earth Guild, Inc. Dept. S
Hot Springs, N.C. 28743

Greentree Ranch Wools
163 North Carter Lake Rd.
Loveland, Colo. 80537

Robin & Russ, Handweavers
533 North Adams St.
McMinnville, Ore. 97128

Specialists in Craft Books

(Their catalogs give excellent descriptions of their books.)

The Unicorn
Craft & Hobby Book Service
Box 645
Rockville, Md. 20851

Museum Books
48 East 43rd St.
New York, N.Y. 10017

Tools

Living Designs
313 South Murphy
Sunnyvale, Calif. 94086
(Navaho tools, yarns)

Gallagher Tools
318 Pacheco Ave.
Santa Cruz, Calif. 95062
(Handmade wooden tools)

Schacht Spindle Co.
1708 Walnut Ave.
Boulder, Colo. 80302

School Products Co.
1201 Broadway
New York, N.Y. 10001
(Metal rigid heddle, various widths)

Dryad
Northgates,
Leicester, England
(Metlyx Heddles, various widths)

Especially for yarns

The Yarn Depot
545 Sutter St.
San Francisco, Calif. 94102

Berga/Ullman
59 Demond Ave.
North Adams, Mass. 02147

Stanley Berroco
140 Mendon St.
Uxbridge, Mass. 01569

The Mannings Weavers Supply Center
R D No. 2
East Berlin, Pa. 17316

William Condon & Sons
203 Fitzroy St.
Charlottestown
Prince Edward Island
C1A 3S2 Canada

Dyestuffs

Glen Black Handwoven Textiles
1414 Grant Ave.
San Francisco, Calif. 94133

Dharma Trading
1952 University Ave.
Berkeley, Calif. 94701

Straw Into Gold
Box 2904S
Oakland, Calif. 94618

Kasuri Dyeworks
1959 Shattuck Ave.
Berkeley, Calif. 94701

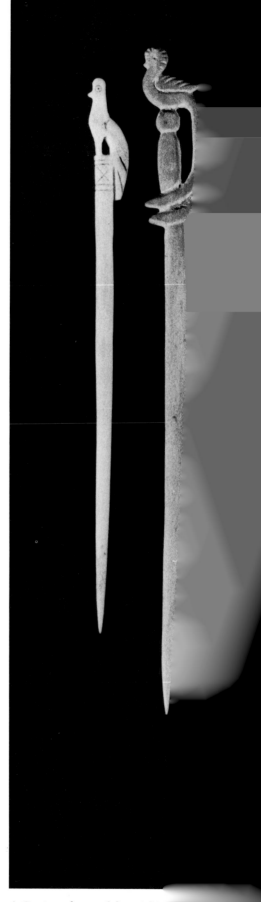

*A Guatemalan tool for picki
patterns. These are tradition
decorated with the Quetzal*

Magazines

The advertisements in these magazines will always be found to contain up-to-date sources for weaving materials, as well as articles you might enjoy. Look them up in your local library, for they are seldom seen on newsstands. You might send for a single copy.

Shuttle, Spindle and Dyepot is the quarterly magazine of the Handweavers Guild of America, 998 Farmington Ave., West Hartford, Conn., 06107.

The Handweavers Guild also publishes an annual *Suppliers Directory,* listing hundreds of suppliers.

Fiberarts, 50 College St., Asheville, N.C., 28801.

A more general magazine is *American Craft* (formerly *Craft Horizons*), published by the American Craft Council, 22 West 55th St., New York, N.Y., 10019.

Books

Books are tools for the mind. Now that you have used this book, there are many possible directions you might pursue. Here are some suggestions; their bibliographies will lead you on to many more.

On Making and Doing

Atwater, Mary Meigs. *Byways in Handweaving.* New York: MacMillan and Co., 1954. Ethnographic techniques from all over, using simple looms.
Bennett, Noel, and Tiana Bighorse. *Working with the Wool: How to Weave a Navaho Rug.* Flagstaff, Arizona: Northland Press, 1971.
Birrel, Verla. *The Textile Arts.* New York: Harper and Row, 1959. Encyclopedic information.
Brooklyn Botanic Garden. *Dyeplant and Dyeing: A Handbook.* Vol. 20, no. 3 of "Plants and Gardens." Brooklyn, N.Y., 1964.
Cason, Marjory, and Adele Cahlander. *The Art of Bolivian Highland Weaving.* New York: Watson-Guptill, 1976. The traditional techniques, finger-by-finger.
D'Harcourt, Raoul. *Textiles of Ancient Peru and Their Techniques.* Edited by Grace G. Denny and Carolyn M. Osborne. Translated by Sadie Brown. Seattle: University of Washington Press, 1974. Complex ancient webs analyzed.
Held, Shirley B. *Weaving: A Handbook for Fiber Craftsmen.* New York: Holt, Rinehart, and Winston, 1973.
Jayne, Caroline Furness. *String Figures and How to Make Them.* New York: Dover Press, 1962.
Russ, Steven. *Fabric Printing by Hand.* New York: Watson-Guptill, 1965. Information about different dye-types.
Trotzig, Liv, and Astrid Axelsson. *Weaving Bands.* Translated by Marianne Turner. New York: Van Nostrand Reinhold, 1974. Very Scandinavian, many patterns.
Znamierowski, Nell. *Step-by-Step Weaving.* New York: Golden Press, 1967. Introductory text, a good start on floor-loom weaving.

On Thinking about It

Albers, Anni. *On Designing.* New Haven, Conn: Pelango Press, 1959.
Emery, Irene. *The Primary Structures of Fabrics.* Washington, D.C.: The Textile Museum, 1966. An encyclopedic scholarly analysis.
Pye, David. *The Nature and Art of Workmanship.* New York: Van Nostrand Reinhold, 1971.

People Who Weave and Their Work

Beskow, Elsa. *Pelle's New Suit.* Translated by Marion Letcher Woodburn. New York: Harper and Row, 1929. A Swedish child's story, all the steps from fleece to clothes.

Constantine, Mildred, and Jack Lenor Larsen. *Beyond Craft: The Art Fabric.* New York: Van Nostrand Reinhold, 1972. A "museum trip" through modern handweaving.

Cordry, Donald, and Dorothy Cordry. *Mexican Indian Costume.* Austin: University of Texas Press, 1968.

Gilpin, Laura. *The Enduring Navaho.* Austin: University of Texas Press, 1968.

Jenness, Aylette, and Lisa W. Kroeber. *A Life of Their Own: An Indian Family in Latin America.* New York: Thomas Crowell, 1975. An account of a Guatemalan family and the part weaving plays in their lives.

Kahlenberg, Mary Hunt, and Anthony Berlant. *The Navaho Blanket.* New York: Praeger, 1968.

Larsen, Jack Lenor. *The Dyer's Art: Ikat, Batik, Plangi.* New York: Van Nostrand Reinhold, 1976.

Pettersen, Carmen Lind. *Maya of Guatemala: Life and Dress.* Seattle: University of Washington Press, 1976.

Rossback, Ed. *Baskets as Textile Art.* New York: Van Nostrand Reinhold, 1973.

Rowe, Ann Pollard. *Warp-Patterned Weaves of the Andes.* Washington, D.C.: The Textile Museum, 1977.

Sieber, Roy. *African Textiles and Decorative Arts.* New York: Museum of Modern Art, 1973.